A Sourcebook for
Teaching Problem Solving

A Sourcebook for Teaching Problem Solving

Stephen Krulik
Temple University

Jesse A. Rudnick
Temple University

Allyn and Bacon, Inc.
Boston London Sydney Toronto

Library of Congress Cataloging in Publication Data

Krulik, Stephen.
  A sourcebook for teaching problem solving.

  1. Problem solving—Study and teaching.   I. Rudnick,
Jesse A.   II. Title.
BF441.K78 1984   153.4'3   83-15746
ISBN 0-205-08106-1

Printed in the United States of America

10 9 8 7 6 5 4   87

Contents

CHAPTER 1

Introduction

It is widely accepted that problem solving is an important basic skill. Indeed, to many people, problem solving is the primary goal of mathematics instruction. Support for this position was given by the National Council of Supervisors of Mathematics in 1977 when they placed problem solving as the number one basic skill in their published list of the ten basic skills of mathematics. Then, in 1980, the National Council of Teachers of Mathematics stated in their publication, *An Agenda for Action,* that problem solving must be the focus of school mathematics in the 1980s.

In this rapidly moving technological age in which we find ourselves, it is difficult to predict what kinds of mathematics will be required of our young people when they take their place in society. Indeed, with the growth and development of electronic calculators and computers it is entirely possible that much of our current school mathematics will be outmoded. This seems entirely likely with regard to many of the computational and manipulative tasks that are presently occupying substantial time.

One topic, however, seems to remain constant, and that is problem solving. Regardless of the time and available technology, people will always have to resolve problems. Whether they face them at work or at play, face them they must! Even the computer must be programmed and the proper buttons on the calculator pressed if these tools are to provide the correct answers. The technology can find answers but only the human mind can solve problems. Problem solving is the primary skill that our students must take with them when they leave our classrooms and enter the "real world."

Yes, most of us agree that problem solving is a vital skill. But how to impart this skill to our students? That is the question with which this book deals. It contains specific activities which teachers can use to develop the problem solving abilities of their students.

WHAT IS A PROBLEM?

To many of our colleagues, the terms "question," "exercise," and "problem" are often used synonymously. And yet, they are quite different. What is a problem for one student may well be an exercise or a question for another. For example, let's look at the following:

$$7 \times 8 = ?$$

If we ask this of students in the ninth or tenth grades, we expect an immediate response of "56." We are testing their memory. To these students,

$7 \times 8 = ?$ is a *question*; it requires a simple *recall* of facts, of something previously learned.

If we ask this of a student in the third or fourth grade, after they have learned the meaning of multiplication, we are providing them with drill and practice to help them commit the facts to memory. We are now talking about an *exercise*; the use of *drill and practice* to reinforce a newly learned fact or concept.

If we now ask this of a youngster in the first or second grade, and the youngster thinks about it, realizes that 7×8 means finding the total number of objects there are in seven groups each containing eight objects, then we are dealing with *complex thought processes*. For this youngster 7×8 is a *problem*.

In other words,

question → immediate recall, memory
exercise → drill and practice
problem → thought, synthesis of knowledge

Notice that what is a problem for one person, may be an exercise or a question for another. In fact, at different stages of a person's mathematical development, the same example may be a question, an exercise, or a problem.

The formal definition of a problem which we will use throughout this book is the following:

A *problem* is a situation, quantitative or otherwise, that confronts an individual or group of individuals, that requires resolution, and for which the individual sees no apparent or obvious means or path to obtaining a solution.[1]

WHAT IS PROBLEM SOLVING?

Using this idea of a problem, *problem solving* emerges as a process. In fact,

It (problem solving) is the means by which an individual uses previously acquired knowledge, skills, and understanding to satisfy the demands of an unfamiliar situation.[2]

And, as a process, problem solving involves a set of skills which can and should be taught. Perhaps the best way to identify the components of this process, is to examine the flow chart shown in Figure 1.1. This flow chart is a pictorial representation of the problem-solving process. It shows the stages a problem solver goes through in resolving a problem, together with many of the subskills that facilitate the solution.

---

[1] Stephen Krulik and Jesse A. Rudnick, *Problem Solving: A Handbook For Teachers* (Boston: Allyn and Bacon, Inc., 1980) 3.
[2] Ibid.

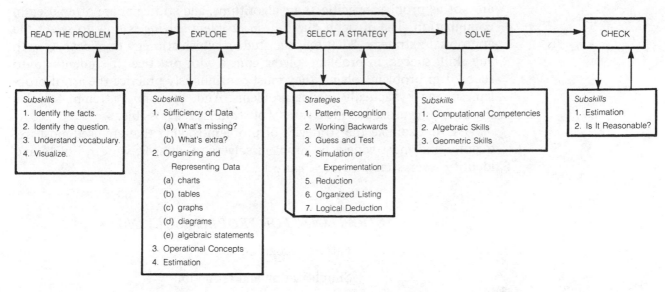

Figure 1.1

THE STRATEGIES OF PROBLEM SOLVING

The heuristics we use in problem solving differ markedly from the algorithms we teach in our mathematics classrooms. An *algorithm* guarantees success if applied correctly and if the proper algorithm has been selected. The *heuristics* shown by the flow chart in Figure 1.1 constitute a five-step approach to problem solving that we feel should be developed and emphasized with children:

1. Read the problem
2. Explore
3. Select a strategy
4. Solve the problem
5. Review, look back, extend the solution

These heuristics provide a "road map;" they are a blueprint that directs your path towards the solution and resolution of a problem situation. Unlike an algorithm, they cannot guarantee success! However, if our students are taught to follow these heuristics in *every* problem situation they face, then they will be in a good position to resolve successfully the problems they will face in the classroom and in life. Again, let us emphasize that while we do want students to complete successfully the solution of a problem and find the required answer, it is the problem-solving process that we emphasize in this book.

The third heuristic on the list, "Select a strategy," is considered by most people to be the most difficult heuristic of all. A *strategy* is that part of the problem-solving process which provides the direction the problem solver should take in finding the answer. Its selection is suggested by the reading and exploration phases that precede it in the heuristic plan. Strategies are not as problem-specific as are algorithms, and strategies are often used in combination. The difficult question in problem solving is how to select the appropriate strategy. What tells the student which strategy to select? As with any skill, success in problem solving comes with practice. If students are to succeed in problem solving, they must continuously practice the art of problem solving by actually solving problems. And, they must attempt to solve the problems using as wide a variety of strategies as possible.

If we examine the strategies of problem solving that are used most frequently and most widely by problem solvers of all ages, we can isolate and identify seven strategies (see Figure 1.2):

STRATEGIES FOR PROBLEM SOLVING

Pattern recognition

Simplification and reduction

Experimentation and simulation

Guess and test

Logical deduction

Organized listing

Working backwards

Figure 1.2

It is these strategies that should be emphasized as the students engage in the problem-solving activities included in this book, as well as in those they face under other conditions.

THE SUBSKILLS OF PROBLEM SOLVING

In addition to proper strategy selection, successful problem solving depends upon the possession and utilization of a series of subskills as shown in Figure 1.3. Much of the research in problem solving indicates that mastery of these subskills will increase overall performance in problem solving. Subskills are a combination of verbal and mathematical skills which enable a student to analyze a problem and understand it. We know, for example, that the subskills of problem solving, if used in combination, will help provide a solution to a problem.

A successful procedure will involve combinations of these subskills to generate the information needed to attack the problem. Then, too, using the subskills as the building blocks of problem solving will often result in combinations that become more meaningful and more effective as the student "sharpens" these subskills. Students need many opportunities to practice the subskills. This book will provide material to do just that.

THE SUBSKILLS OF PROBLEM SOLVING

1. Identifying facts
2. Identifying questions
3. Understanding vocabulary
4. Visualization
5. What's missing
6. What's extra
7. Organizing and representing data
   Tables
   Diagrams
   Charts
   Graphs
8. Estimation
   Numerical, visual
   Is it reasonable?
9. Algebraic skills
10. Geometric skills

Figure 1.3

HOW TO USE THIS BOOK

It is apparent that the teacher who believes in problem solving as a major goal of teaching mathematics will teach differently from the teacher who does not. Changing to an active focus on problem solving in any mathematics classroom requires a re-evaluation of the instructional goals, instructional time, and evaluation techniques to be used.

Since it is the thought processes that are so important in problem solving (and not merely the answers), and since critical thinking takes time, careful planning must be undertaken.

You should plan on integrating problem solving into your everyday mathematics classes. Problem solving is not a process that can be taught in one week or one month and then ignored. Rather, it must permeate the entire classroom atmosphere, the very way that we teach. It should be actively pursued throughout the student's career in mathematics, with an ever increasing degree of skill and expertise. Above all, *your students must practice problem solving in order to succeed at it!*

This book is organized according to the heuristics. The subskills have been grouped along with the appropriate heuristics. Each chapter of the book is independent of the others. That is, they may be undertaken in any order. As you examine each of the chapters, you will find a series of activities, games, and references to Reproduction Pages. These Reproduction Pages provide materials that you can use immediately with your students to develop their abilities within each subskill. Each subskill is important by itself; together they all contribute to the problem-solving process.

To use the book, decide upon which subskill of problem solving you wish to help your students master at a particular time. You may or may not decide to follow the suggested order by chapters. As you read through each chapter, you will find activities which involve the Reproduction Pages and others which do not. The text material will suggest some ways to approach the materials, and what you can expect to achieve as a result of using them. In addition, directions for using each activity are included. If the activity you wish to use has associated Reproduction Pages, select the one you wish to use. Remove the page, duplicate copies for each student and have them work through as a group/individual activity.

Many of the activities are designed for use with small groups. You will have to decide whether small group means one, three or five students, or even more. In some cases, the entire class will serve as "the group." Your role will vary from activity to activity. Many of them are self-directed and can be used for individual students on their own, with minimal input from you. Others require extensive teacher direction and/or participation. Some will require repetition throughout the school year to be most effective. In some cases, the activity will suggest others which you can develop on your own for further exploration with the students.

In preparing a book such as this one, it is often difficult to discriminate exactly between what is suitable for students at the elementary level, the junior high/middle school level, and the senior high school level. Fortunately, in problem solving many of these arbitrary divisions are unnecessary. As a result, we have not designated any grade level for much of the material. You will have to examine each Reproduction Page within a specific subskill and see if it is suitable for your own personal situation. What we *have* done is to make them span as wide an ability level as possible. That is, in many cases you will find three or more Reproduction Pages designed to improve a single subskill at two or three different levels. Since these are arbitrary selections, you will notice that the levels often overlap in content. We cannot stress enough the role *you* must play in selecting the activities best suited for your own classes. Don't be misled by any grade indications—no one knows your classes as well as you do! Select those materials which you feel are best suited for your students and use them! Then, if you want still more practice, create more of them in a similar manner for your own use.

HOW TO EVALUATE PROBLEM-SOLVING ACTIVITIES

As we have already indicated, evaluation methods for problem solving will have to be more flexible and more varied than for many other kinds of instructional tasks. Since we are assessing a *process*, written instruments are difficult to utilize. Instead, you will have to use subjective data to evaluate students' growth. Realize that problem solving involves "risk taking" on the part of your students. For some students, merely taking such a risk is tremendous growth, a major jump forward. At the same time, the frustrations, perseverance and tenacity that are all a part of problem solving should be evaluated. As a result, you will have to place more of an emphasis on nonnumerical growth, than on standardized tests.

CHAPTER 2

Read the Problem

A major goal of mathematics instruction is to develop in students the ability to solve problems. The traditional manner of presenting problems to students is in verbalized form, either written or oral. If a student cannot read a problem with understanding, he or she can hardly be expected to continue to a reasonable solution.

Successful problem solvers are those who can visualize the setting and gather the important data from the problem as it is written. We must realize that with most students, full comprehension of a problem does not take place all at once, but may take place in stages. That is, the first reading results in only a general familiarity with the setting of the problem. The second reading will begin to allow students to think about the specifics, the relevant data and important facts in a problem. Further readings may lead to strategy selection based on previous experiences in problem solving.

In this chapter, we will focus on activities that will help students increase their ability to read, to understand and to interpret a problem presented in a verbal or written format. It is rare that a teacher can err by giving too much practice to students in reading mastery within subject matter areas; the error is usually the other way around.

Activity 2.1

Fundamental to solving problems that are presented in verbal form is an understanding of the setting and situation described. The problem setting must be familiar to the students. Otherwise, it becomes an exercise in abstraction. At this time, abstraction may be beyond the students' ability level. Indeed, it adds a complication which interferes with problem solving.

Give the students ample opportunity to read a problem and identify the setting and pieces of information that are contained therein. Reproduction Pages 1–3, which we call "What's Going On?," provide practice in this important subskill.

Activity 2.2

Have students restate problems in their own words. Sometimes this will not only help the problem solver begin his or her deliberations, but the restatement of the problem will help him or her visualize what is taking place. The class should serve as a reviewing team to make certain the reader has included all of the information from the problem. Questions directed to the reader by the class will help in this effort. Use problems similar to those on Reproduction Pages 1–3. Have one student describe the problem in his or her own words.

Activity 2.3

Research has shown that the ability to recognize words is fundamental to reading. Since reading is a vital part of problem solving, any expansion of the ability to read will assist in the development of problem-solving skills.

Reproduction Pages 4, 5, and 6 provide experiences in word recognition. The task assigned to the students is simply to match words. Upon completion of the exercise, we recommend that the meanings of the words be discussed.

Activity 2.4

When problems are presented in written form, many students experience trouble because they misinterpret some words which have multiple meanings depending upon context. There are many words that have different meanings when they are used in non-mathematical situations and when they are used in mathematics. For example, the word "prime" when used in mathematics refers to a number which has only itself and one as factors. In the non-mathematical sense, "prime" can refer to special or choice, as in "a prime cut of meat" or "prime time television programming." In still another context we can use "prime" as a verb and refer to "prime the pump" to get it started.

It may be that some of our students will recognize a word they have encountered in their everyday reading. We often assume that, because they recognize a word, they are using its mathematical meaning in a problem. This may not be true. In fact, students may impose the non-mathematical meaning and thus completely lose the sense of the problem. Reproduction Pages 7 and 8 provide students with practice in identifying words with multiple meanings.

In Reproduction Page 7, we provide a list of words which have more than one meaning. This list is followed by pairs of sentences which illustrate both the mathematical and the non-mathematical meanings. The students should look through the list and select the one word that fits into both blanks in each pair.

In Reproduction Page 8, the procedure is the same except that we have not provided the list of words for the students. These must be drawn upon from memory.

One valuable extension of this activity is to have students keep a mathematics dictionary. Whenever a new word is discovered that has a double meaning, have the students write it in their dictionaries with both meanings and then write a sentence to illustrate each.

Activity 2.5

Every problem consists basically of two parts: facts and questions. Students cannot solve problems unless they can identify the question being asked. Reproduction Pages 9–11 are designed to help your students discover "What's The Question?"

In Reproduction Page 9, students are to read each problem and select the proper question.

In Reproduction Page 10, the students are to read each problem and underline the question.

In Reproduction Page 11, the students are to supply an appropriate question for each problem.

Activity 2.6

Students must also be able to determine the important facts in a problem. These facts can be presented in a variety of ways, including picture form, and paragraph or written form. Reproduction Pages 12 and 13 provide pictures followed by a series of questions. Students should answer the questions by finding the facts in the picture.

Reproduction Pages 14 and 15 provide paragraphs of text material with the important facts imbedded in the text. Students are to read the material and answer each question that follows.

Activity 2.7

The analysis of a problem is a vital part of the problem-solving process. We feel that an added dimension to this analysis would be provided if students were given an opportunity to create problems on their own. In this activity (Reproduction Pages 16–18) the students are asked to create problem situations which fit solutions already presented. They must provide problems which involve a reasonable choice of numbers. The student should be certain the problem he or she has created results in the given answer.

Activity 2.8

This activity is designed to sharpen the students' ability to read a problem with comprehension. Pair the students in your class, and designate one as the "Problem Reader" and the other as the "Problem Solver."

The Problem Readers are then presented the problem visually, via an overhead projector, for a limited time period (15–30 seconds). During this time, the Problem Solver is not permitted to view the screen. The reader can make any notes—written or mental—that he or she wishes during this time period. At the end of the visual period, the readers present the problem to their solvers, who attempt to solve the problem.

Reverse the students' roles and go through the procedure again.

Activity 2.9

A fun activity that enables children to be creative is to present them with a series of pictures similar to those on Reproduction Pages 19-21. These should stimulte problems. Let each student write a problem inspired by the setting of the picture. Have each problem presented to the class for solution.

Save these problems, since many of them will be interesting and can be used in future classroom situations.

A word of warning: our experience has revealed that many of the problems developed by children contain numbers that make no sense within the problem setting. Of course this activity is intended to bring the sense of realism to the children's attention.

CHAPTER 3

Explore

The second heuristic in the problem-solving process is "EXPLORE." Thus, after a child has had sufficient practice in reading with comprehension, he or she should have experience in organizing in an orderly fashion the data presented in a problem. A careful organization and analysis of data will often reveal a strategy which in turn leads to the answer.

In this chapter, we present several activities designed to produce a variety of experiences in organizing and analyzing data. The activities also provide experiences with determining data sufficiency.

Activity 3.1

Here is an activity in which the students are asked to differentiate between necessary and unnecessary information. Successful problem solving depends upon this ability. Often problems contain distractors which obscure the solution by masking the important information. Reproduction Pages 22–25 will provide an opportunity for students to discriminate between necessary and unnecessary information.

Activity 3.2

There are actually two different skills involved in working with tables. One is interpreting data that is presented in tabular form, and the other is developing a table to illustrate information given in a problem.

Reproduction Pages 26–30 provide several different kinds of tables, each followed by a series of questions. Students should abstract the data from the table and answer each question.

Reproduction Pages 31–35 present a series of problems for which students should complete tables that have been started and/or construct their own appropriate tables.

ON YOUR OWN

Involving students in creating their own problems is a powerful motivational idea. We recommend that you have groups of students develop surveys. Have them develop a questionnaire and conduct the survey in the school or in the neighborhood. Have them prepare a table and/or a graph to illustrate the data collected. They should then exchange their tables or graphs and answer questions similar to those shown on Reproduction Pages 26–35.

Some possible surveys might include:

- the number of hours students watch television every day;
- determining students' favorites, in areas such as sports, foods, cars, ice cream flavors, etc.;
- traffic surveys to include such things as the number of foreign versus domestic cars; body styles (4-door, 2-door); car colors; women drivers versus men drivers; even-numbered license plates versus odd-numbered license plates.

Activity 3.3

Closely related to tables as a means of organizing data are graphs. Reproduction Pages 36–40 present bar, line and circle graphs, followed by questions which the students should answer directly from the information on the graph. Reproduction Pages 41–44 contain problems for which the students should draw appropriate graphs. They should solve each of the problems utilizing their graphs.

Activity 3.4

Another way to effectively represent data is to draw a sketch or diagram. Diagrams can enter into problem-solving strategies in several ways. First of all, there are many cases in which the problem is presented as a diagram. Problems in geometry, in networks, partitioning and mazes are examples of these. Secondly, diagrams help to visualize the given data or to display some of the important characteristics and relationships that exist within the problem.

Diagrams also can be used to illustrate various kinds of action contained in some problems, such as problems of motion, exchanging goods or mixtures. A properly developed diagram will often lead directly to the final answer.

See that the students have ample experiences with constructing diagrams, even though an alternate solution may be suggested. Drawing a diagram is an important subskill and requires a great deal of practice. Reproduction Pages 45–48 provide problems for which diagrams should be drawn. (Note: Problem 1 on Reproduction Page 47 can be solved by using a Venn diagram.)

Activity 3.5

Probably the most powerful problem-solving skill is the ability to represent symbolically a problem situation. If a student can represent the verbal information in symbolic or algebraic form, then he or she has done much of the problem analysis needed to clear the path to an answer. Reproduction Pages 49–53 give students the opportunity to analyze verbal expressions and represent them with mathematical symbols and vice versa.

CHAPTER 4

Choosing and Using Strategies

We come now to the most crucial stage of problem solving, that of choosing and using strategies. In Chapter 1 we identified seven widely used strategies. This is far from an exhaustive list, nor are the seven strategies distinct. However, the ability to recognize and use these seven will enhance the problem-solving abilities of our students. Even if these strategies are not specifically used, at least they provide a springboard to the selection of one that will lead to the desired answer.

Strategy selection is difficult! For a few students, knowing what strategy to use in a specific problem comes about intuitively. (In fact, these fortunate few are unaware of why or how they chose to do what they did.) For most of us, however, proper strategy selection is the result of repeated exposure to lots and lots of problems.

The activities that follow are intended to provide practice for your students. We have divided these activities by strategies along with associated subskills. Remember, there is a great divergence among students in their ability to analyze and select proper strategies. This ability does not necessarily correlate with computational skill. Thus class time must be devoted to the discussion of the problem, and various approaches to a solution. Each child's contribution, even though it might appear to be completely irrelevant, should be considered because even blind paths contribute to the development of the elusive skill we are attempting to build.

Many of the Reproduction Pages referred to in this chapter will merely contain problems. These can be distributed to students for practice. However, each problem is discussed in the text. It is important that you spend sufficient time discussing the solution as well as the answer to each problem, emphasizing the choice of strategy.

The first strategy we have chosen to discussion is *pattern recognition*.

PATTERN RECOGNITION

Recognizing patterns is a skill that must be developed by students. In fact, many mathematicians say the art of mathematics is the search for patterns. Patterns appear in many forms. There are patterns of numbers. There are patterns of form. There can be patterns of letters and patterns of words. School mathematics programs contain an abundance of number patterns. It is our feeling that exposure to other pattern forms as well, will enhance the students' sensitivity and the ability to recognize patterns.

Many of us take for granted that children see patterns just because they are obvious to us. In fact, many of these children see nothing at all! The patterns must be pointed out as well as the rule by which the pattern is developed. Direct experiences with pattern search must be included as an integral part of school mathematics.

Activity 4.1

This activity, consisting of Reproduction Pages 54–56, gives students experience with a variety of patterns.

Reproduction Page 54 covers patterns determined by affinity groups. For example, in the first question, the affinity group is fruits, while in question 2, the group is colors. Question 6 contains even numbers, while question 11 contains fractions.

Reproduction Page 55 deals with traditional sequential patterns. One of the more non-routine sequences is number 4, where each word is sequenced according to the number of letters that appear in it; i.e., first word—one letter, second word—two letters, and so on. Notice that in question 7, two factors are involved: the words are sequenced by the alphabetic order of the first letters, and the alternating of girls' names and boys' names. In question 11, the sequence is determined by the first letter of the months of the year.

Reproduction Page 56 is a combination of Pages 54 and 55. The question asked of the students is to determine which of the given elements does not belong in the affinity group and/or which one is out of sequence. Number 5 contains all names of rock groups, except for the Dodgers (a baseball team). Number 10 shows legal holidays as they occur throughout the calendar year; Halloween is not a legal holiday.

Activity 4.2

This activity, Reproduction Page 57, asks students to examine geometric sequences, and determine the next two terms. We have set this activity apart because the sequences all involve geometric figures, rather than the alphanumeric ones in the previous activity.

Activity 4.3

Reproduction Pages 58 and 59 involve analogous reasoning. That is, the students are given two figures (Column A and B) that are related. Using this relationship, they are asked to find the mate to a figure given in Column C amongst the figures in Columns 1–4.

This kind of question often appears on standardized tests of mathematical aptitude. It will probably be necessary to discuss at some length these analogies because, more than likely, the students will have had little or no previous experience with them.

Activity 4.4

Activities 4.1, 4.2, and 4.3 were intended to develop student facility in pattern recognition. This activity presents several problems whose solutions center upon pattern recognition. Note that most problems are not resolved by merely observing patterns, but utilize other strategies as well. We will present a few problems here that *are* nicely solved by the use of pattern recognition, but in the sections that follow pattern recognition will be combined with other strategies.

Problem (Reproduction Page 60)

My grandmother likes apples, but dislikes oranges. She likes beef, but dislikes lamb. She likes teenagers, but dislikes children. She likes parrots, but dislikes cats and dogs. She likes cookies, but dislikes cakes and pies.

Which of the following would you say my grandmother likes?

OBJECT	LIKES	DISLIKES
pears		
veal		
copper		
brass		
bitter fruits		
sweet chocolate		
hot chocolate		
cool weather		
oceans		
swimming pool		

Figure 4.1

Discussion

Grandmother's likes and dislikes should be recorded in a two-column table:

Likes	Dislikes
apples	oranges
beef	lamb
teenagers	children
parrots	cats
cookies	dogs
	cakes
	pies

This will enable the students to examine the separate lists for commonalities. After much deliberation, the students should notice that each word in the "Likes" column contains a double letter. This attribute does not appear in the words in the "Dislikes" column. Notice that the actual meaning of the word is not involved; it is the word itself that holds the key.

This is a verbal situation that is analogous to the number versus numeral distinction that is often discussed in elementary mathematics.

Problem (Reproduction Page 61)

My grandfather likes beef, but dislikes veal. He likes an abacus, but dislikes a calculator. He likes towels marked "HIS" and "HERS." He likes to sigh, but never to cry. He likes calm people, but he dislikes angry people. He likes Houston, but dislikes Dallas.

Which of the following would you say my grandfather likes?

OBJECT	LIKES	DISLIKES
stamps		
ferryboats		
tugboats		
Chinese food		
Mexican food		
notepaper		
gold		
flashlight		
rust		
roses		

Figure 4.2

Discussion

As in the previous problem, my grandfather's likes and dislikes should be placed in a table. (This technique illustrates the importance of the table format for problem solving.) The key to the solution in this problem lies in that each word in the "LIKES" column contains two consecutive letters in the alphabet, a fact that does not appear in the "DISLIKES" column. (For example, be*ef*, *ab*acus, Hou*st*on, etc.)

Problem (Reproduction Page 62)

Dolores and Pat started a pen pal club. It was decided that once a month each member would send a letter to every member of the club. It was also decided to add one new member to the club each month. How many letters were mailed during the month in which the sixth member joined the club?

Discussion

The situation should be illustrated with a series of diagrams as shown in Figure 4.3. The information gained should be recorded in a table.

  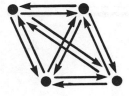

Figure 4.3

Number of members	Number of letters
2	2
3	6
4	12
5	20
6	30

Problem (Reproduction Page 63)

The REC Record Company just released a new album. The first week, they only received two orders. Then the album began to catch on. The second week they received 27 orders; the third week they received 57 orders; the fourth week they received 92 orders. At this same rate, how many orders will they receive the sixth week?

Discussion

Again, the information should be recorded in a two-column table:

Week number	Number of orders	
1	2	
2	27	> 25
3	57	> 30
4	92	> 35

SIMPLIFICATION AND REDUCTION

Realistic problems often contain very large numbers or a great many cases. These complex number and multiple case situations tend to obscure the procedures and arithmetic processes needed for the problem solution. The problem can be greatly simplified but remain mathematically unaltered, if smaller numbers are substituted and/or the number of cases reduced. For example, if a factory manufactures 750,287 circuit boards at a cost of $14.75 per unit, to find the entire product cost presents a much more difficult task to the student than if the numbers were simplified to 5 circuit boards at $2 each.

Activity 4.5

Here are some problems in which reduction and/or simplification should be used.

Problem

The attendance at the final game of the state-wide soccer tournament was 22,478. The concession stands took in $39,336.50. What was the average amount spent by each person at the game?

Discussion

These numbers are horrendous! A student could easily be confused and frightened by their magnitude. He or she might even refuse to go any further. If the numbers were reduced to 100 people who spent $200, the student would see that the problem is a simple average problem which requires division. The answer is obtained by dividing the amount taken in by the concessionaires by the number of people in attendance. In the simplified problem, this is merely $200 ÷ 100 people. In the original problem this extends to $39,336.50 ÷ 22,478 people. The use of a hand-held calculator would be most appropriate.

The previous problem was one in which the arithmetic data consisted of large numbers. The following problem illustrates a form of reduction, one in which the number of cases should be reduced.

Problem   (Reproduction Page 64)

In the intramural bowling tournament, there are 16 entries. The tournament is a single match elimination; that is, two bowlers compete at a time, and the loser is eliminated. How many games will be bowled to determine the champion?

Discussion

Obviously, the use of 16 is an arbitrary decision. Why not start with two bowlers? Then only one game would be needed. If the number of bowlers is increased to three, then the number of games needed would be two. (The winner of the first match bowls against the third bowler.) Similarly, four bowlers would require three matches. (The winner of the first match bowls against the winner of the second match.) Record this information in a table:

Number of bowlers	2	3	4
Number of games	1	2	3

The student should quickly see that, regardless of the number of bowlers, the number of games required is one less than the number of bowlers.

Problem

How thick is a single sheet of mimeograph paper?

Discussion

To measure a single sheet of mimeograph paper would require the use of a micrometer. A simpler problem (simpler in terms of method) would be to measure the thickness of a ream of mimeograph paper and divide by 500 (the number of sheets of paper in the ream). The ream of paper is five centimeters thick; thus a single sheet of paper would be 5/500 or .01 cm or 1 mm thick.

Problem (Reproduction Page 65)

How many squares are there on a standard 8 X 8 checkerboard?

Discussion

The students' first reaction to this problem is to say "64 squares." However, it soon becomes apparent that there are considerably more than 64 when one considers the number of 2 X 2 squares, 3 X 3 squares, 4 X 4 squares, etc. This problem can best be done by a combination of reduction and making a table.

NUMBER OF SQUARES

Size board	1X1	2X2	3X3	4X4	5X5	6X6	7X7	8X8	Total
1 X 1	1	–	–	–	–	–	–	–	1
2 X 2	4	1	–	–	–	–	–	–	5
3 X 3	9	4	1	–	–	–	–	–	14
4 X 4	16	9	4	1	–	–	–	–	30
5 X 5									
6 X 6									
7 X 7									
8 X 8									

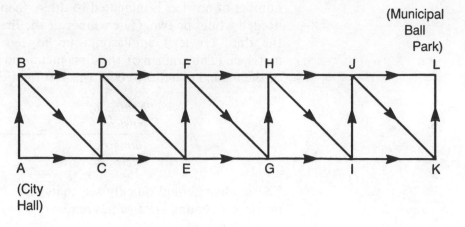

Figure 4.4

Problem   (Reproduction Page 66)

Figure 4.4 is a map of the streets in a city. All of the streets are one way as indicated by the arrows. How many different routes are there to go from City Hall (A) to the Municipal Ball Park (L)?

Discussion

The choice of point L is an arbitrary one. Suppose we go just from A to B. There is only one way to get there (Figure 4.5). How about from A to C? There are two ways (A–B–C and A–C); A to D? Three ways; A to E? Five ways; A to F? Eight ways; and so on.

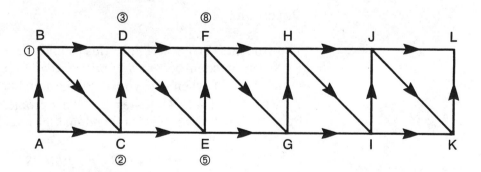

Figure 4.5

This process can be continued until one reaches point L (the ball park), and the number of ways, 144, is revealed.

However, the sequence, 1, 2, 3, 5, 8, ... is the well-known Fibonacci sequence, where each term after the first two is the sum of the previous two terms.

Problem   (Reproduction Page 67)

On a recent vacation trip, the Fernando family drove a total of 3,468 miles. Their car averaged 21.6 miles per gallon, and the average price of a gallon of gasoline was $1.37 9/10. How much did they spend for gasoline on the trip?

Discussion

Since children cringe at problems with large numbers, let's simplify the numbers in this problem. Suppose the trip was 100 miles, they averaged 20 miles per gallon, and gasoline was $1 per gallon. The students could easily see that the family used five gallons of gasoline (100 ÷ 20) and this cost $5 (5 × $1). Using this same format as a model, the original problem can now be solved.

EXPERIMENTATION AND SIMULATION

Some problems lend themselves to *experimentation,* to acting out. That is, the students can best solve the problem by DOING IT! Indeed, acting out the problem forces an understanding of the nature of the problem. If someone is capable of acting out the problem, we can almost be certain that he or she understands it. For example, if a student is asked to determine how many board erasers can be placed end-to-end on the chalk tray of a blackboard in the front of the room, the answer can be obtained by actually lining up board erasers. If a child performs this experiment, he not only will find the answer, but will indicate a complete understanding of the problem.

Another illustration which can *only* be done by experimentation would be to determine how many times you can snap your finger in 20 seconds. This can only be done by actually snapping fingers and counting, while someone else keeps track of time.

On the other hand, some problem situations are impossible to actually carry out. For these, a *simulation* is more practical. Bottle caps can be used in place of snowballs; chips can represent people. Or, we can simulate the action with pencil and paper, by making a drawing or a table.

Activity 4.6

Here are some problems for which experimentation is the solution strategy. Students must act them out.

1. How long does it take for a book to fall from the desk to the floor?
2. How many pennies laid next to each other are needed to measure exactly one foot?
3. How many checkers will fill a one pound coffee can?
4. How many seats are in the auditorium of your school?

5. Are there more boys or more girls in your class?
6. How many people in your class were born in April?
7. Which has more pages, your dictionary or your local telephone directory?
8. How many scoops of ice cream can you get from one-half gallon of vanilla ice cream?
9. Which rock group is the favorite of your class?
10. How long does it take you to read a page of print?
11. Can you run a 100-yard dash faster than a car can drive one-half mile at 55 miles an hour?
12. (Reproduction Page 68) Place 20 pennies on the table in a row. Replace every fourth coin with a nickel. Now replace every third coin with a dime. Now replace every sixth coin with a quarter. What is the value of the 20 coins now on the table?
13. (Reproduction Page 69) Place 20 pennies on the table in a row, with heads up. Now "flip" every coin to show tails. Now "flip" every other coin beginning with the second penny (2, 4, 6, . . .). Now flip every third coin, beginning with the third penny (3, 6, 9, . . .). Next flip every fourth penny, beginning with the fourth coin (4, 8, 12, . . .). Continue this procedure for 20 trials. Which pennies now have the heads up?

Activity 4.7

The previous set of problems were all best done by *experimentation*, by actually doing what the problem called for. Now, here are some problems that should be done by simulating the action.

Problem   (Reproduction Page 70)

There are 20 students collecting golf balls that have fallen into the water trap, and selling them for practice balls. The first student brought in one golf ball. The second student then sold the ball. Student number three brought in three golf balls; student number four then sold one of them. Student number five brought in five golf balls; student number six sold one. Student number seven brought in seven golf balls; student number eight sold one. This continues so that every odd-numbered student brings in the same number of golf balls as his or her number, while the even-numbered students sell one golf ball each. When all 20 students have done their thing, how many golf balls will be in the pile?

Discussion

The students can use bottle caps to simulate the golf balls, or we can simulate the action with a table:

Student	Collects	Sells	Total
1	1	–	1
2	–	1	0
3	3	–	3
4	–	1	2
5	5	–	7
6	–	1	6
7	7	–	13
8	–	1	12
9	9	–	21
10	–	1	20
11	11	–	31
12	–	1	30
13	13	–	43
14	–	1	42
15	15	–	57
16	–	1	56
17	17	–	73
18	–	1	72
19	19	–	91
20	–	1	90

An interesting extension to this problem would be to have students graph the action.

Problem   (Reproduction Page 71)

In a corner of the basement, Julie found an old rectangular fish tank frame; that is, the glass had been removed. An ant on one corner decides to crawl to the opposite corner. In how many different ways can the ant get to the opposite corner by walking along exactly three edges of the frame?

Discussion

This problem can be done by an experiment if we can find an old fish tank. However, a paper and pencil simulation is probably more appropriate (Figure 4.6).

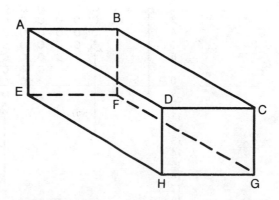

Figure 4.6

The problem now reduces to how many three-edge paths are there from point A to point G.

Problem (Reproduction Page 72)

The new school has exactly 1,000 lockers and exactly 1,000 students. On the first day of school, the students meet outside the building and agree on the following plan: the first student will enter the school and open all of the lockers. The second student will then enter the school and close every locker with an even number (2, 4, 6, 8, . . .). The third student will then "reverse" every third locker (3, 6, 9, 12, . . .). That is, if the locker is closed, he will open it; if the locker is open, he will close it. The fourth student will then reverse every fourth locker, and so on until all 1,000 students in turn have entered the building and reversed the proper lockers. Which lockers will finally remain open?

Discussion

This well-known problem is a beautiful example of a situation that can be resolved through a variety of strategies. First of all, it can actually be performed with 1,000 students and 1,000 lockers. However, this is obviously unreasonable and, in fact, unnecessary. It can be acted out with 100 students and 100 lockers, a reduction. It can be further reduced to 20. This is a size ample enough to observe the pattern.

A more sophisticated approach utilizing the reduction mentioned above would be to simulate the action using coins or bottle caps to represent the lockers, and "flipping" them to represent opening and closing them. Or, you can let students represent the lockers by holding cards with numbers, and turning forwards and backwards as the lockers are reversed.

However, a paper and pencil simulation would be the most efficient, using a chart as shown:

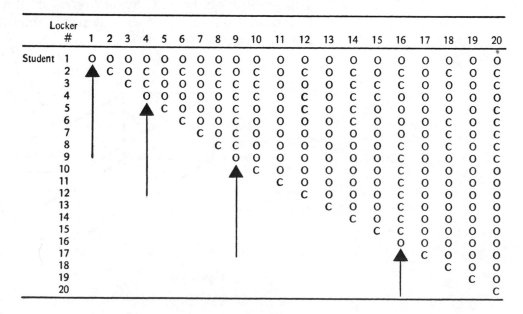

	Locker #																			
Student	1	2	3	4	5	6	7	8	9	10	11	12	13	14	15	16	17	18	19	20
1	O	O	O	O	O	O	O	O	O	O	O	O	O	O	O	O	O	O	O	O
2		C	O	C	O	C	O	C	O	C	O	C	O	C	O	C	O	C	O	C
3			C	C	O	O	O	C	C	C	O	O	O	C	C	C	O	O	O	C
4				O	O	O	O	O	C	C	O	C	O	C	C	O	O	O	O	O
5					C	O	O	O	C	O	O	C	O	C	O	O	O	O	O	C
6						C	O	O	C	O	O	O	O	C	O	O	O	C	O	C
7							C	O	C	O	O	O	O	O	O	O	O	C	O	C
8								C	C	O	O	O	O	O	O	C	O	C	O	C
9									O	O	O	O	O	O	O	C	O	O	O	C
10										C	O	O	O	O	O	C	O	O	O	O
11											C	O	O	O	O	C	O	O	O	O
12												C	O	O	O	C	O	O	O	O
13													C	O	O	C	O	O	O	O
14														C	O	C	O	O	O	O
15															C	C	O	O	O	O
16																O	O	O	O	O
17																	C	O	O	O
18																		C	O	O
19																			C	O
20																				C

All of these require pattern recognition to complete the solution.

The problem is particularly valuable in that it includes some very good mathematical concepts. The key to the solution is the well-known number theoretic property that all numbers have an even number of factors except the perfect squares. The problem also lends itself to a variety of extensions:

1. For a particular locker, how many times was it touched? (The number of factors.)
2. How many lockers, and which ones, were touched exactly twice? (The lockers with prime numbers.)
3. Which locker was touched the most times? (The one with the most factors.)
4. What is the sum of the numbers on all the lockers left open? $\left(\dfrac{N^3}{3} + \dfrac{N^2}{2} + \dfrac{N}{6} \right)$

Problem

In Mr. Lewis's Gym class, 400 students stand in a circle, spaced equally, and numbered consecutively from 1 to 400. Johnny is number 7, and is standing directly opposite Linda. What is Linda's number?

Discussion

The initial obstacle for the students to overcome is for them to understand that "directly opposite" means the endpoints of the diameter of the circle. The problem can be resolved by a combination of reduction and simulation. Reduce the number of students to, say, eight, and draw the circle as in Figure 4.7.

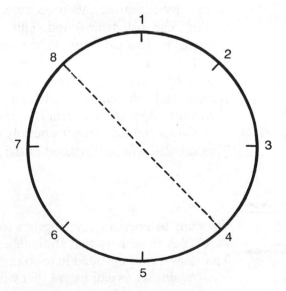

Figure 4.7

This leads to

$$8 \rightarrow 4$$
$$7 \rightarrow 3$$
$$6 \rightarrow 2$$
$$5 \rightarrow 1$$

Now try the problem with 10 students. This will pair up:

$$10 \rightarrow 5$$
$$9 \rightarrow 4$$
$$8 \rightarrow 3$$
$$7 \rightarrow 2$$
$$6 \rightarrow 1$$

The students should realize that an ordinary clock fulfills the conditions of the problem for 12 students. The opposite pairs here are 6 and 12, 5 and 11, 4 and 10, 3 and 9, etc.

The observed pattern is that the difference between the opposite numbers is $N/2$, where N is the total number of people in in the circle. (Note that the problem must be limited to an even number of elements.) Thus, Johnny, number 7, is opposite Linda, number 207.

An extension of this problem is to give the numbers of a pair of opposite students and ask how many are in the circle.

GUESS AND TEST

Probably the most commonly used strategy outside of school is guess and test. In this strategy, one guesses at an answer, then tests the guess to see if it works. By repeating this procedure, the answer, or at least a close approximation, can often be found. This is contrary to traditional teaching, when guessing is frowned upon. Often heard in the classroom is a comment such as, "Do you know, or are you just guessing?" Of course, blind guessing should be discouraged. Guess and test is a viable method in most fields of science and mathematics, where hypotheses are generated (the guess), and then verified by testing them (the test).

Guess and test depends heavily upon the individual's ability to estimate. This subskill will be discussed in the next chapter.

Activity 4.8

We want to encourage youngsters to guess. The Guess Test on Reproduction Page 73 is an activity that students enjoy, and it gives them guessing practice. The answers are included here so they can discuss their guesses.

Again, let us emphasize that wild guesses should be discouraged; guesses must be made within some frame of reference.

Answers to Guess Test

1. 50,000 to 150,000 times
2. 17,600 miles per hour
3. 500–1500 hours
4. 7½ inches
5. about 2,000 pounds
6. answers will vary

7. 17½ feet
8. answers will vary
9. approximately 15 minutes
10. about 700 times
11. the needle moves only about 5 inches

Activity 4.9

Here are some problems that should be done using the guess and test strategy.

Problem   (Reproduction Page 74)

Mary hit the dartboard shown in Figure 4.8 with four darts. Each dart hit a different number. Her total score was 60. How might she have scored 60?

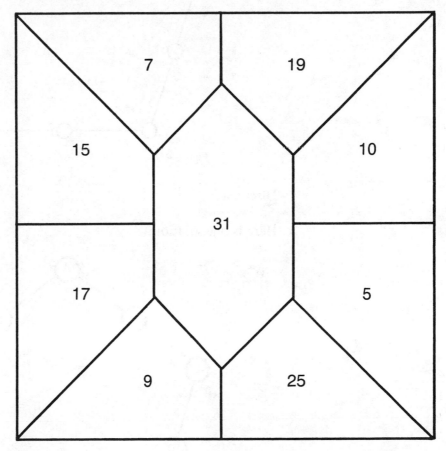

Figure 4.8

Discussion

This problem has more than one solution. However, the answer must contain four odd numbers in order to have an even sum. Two possible solutions are:

$$19 + 17 + 15 + 9 = 60$$
$$31 + 15 + 9 + 5 = 60$$

Problem (Reproduction Page 75)

Fill in the empty circles on each side of the pentagon shown in Figure 4.9 with the numbers from 1–10, so that the sum of the numbers on each side is 14.

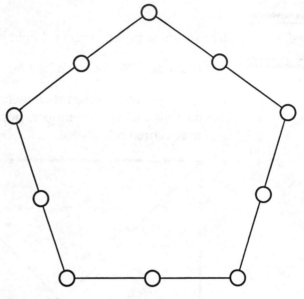

Figure 4.9

Discussion

Here is one solution:

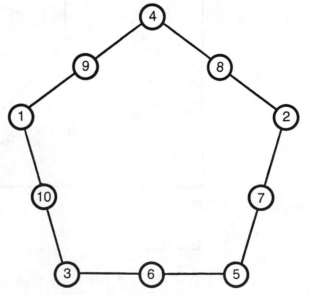

Figure 4.10

Problem

In an effort to motivate his daughter to do her mathematics homework quickly and accurately, a father offered to pay her 8¢ for each correct problem, but to "fine" her 5¢ for each incorrect one. After doing 26 problems, they found that neither owed the other any money. How many problems did the daughter solve correctly?

Discussion

One set of numbers the students might guess could be 5 correct (+ 40¢) and 8 incorrect (− 40¢). This does yield a solution where no one owes any money. However, it only has a total of 13 problems. Doubling this to 10 correct (+ 80¢) and 16 incorrect (− 80¢) gives the solution to the problem.

Problem   (Reproduction Page 76)

Leroy mailed some letters and postcards which cost him a total of $3.85 in postage. If each letter costs 20¢ and each postcard costs 13¢, how many of each did he mail?

Discussion

This problem can be simplified by using refined guessing. Note that $3.85 implies that the number of postcards mailed must end in a "5." Thus the only possible answers for the number of postcards Leroy mailed would be 5, 15, or 25. Testing these guesses yields solutions for both 5 and 25 postcards.

Problem   (Reproduction Page 77)

Alphanumerics are a fun way to practice and refine a guess. A knowledge of arithmetic operations and the properties of numbers is quite helpful.

Discussion

1.   A D A M
       A N D
       E V E
       O N
          A
    ─────────
    R A F T

There are many solutions to this particular problem. Here is one solution that leads to a maximum value:

```
8 3 8 4
  8 0 3
  6 2 6
    5 0
       8
─────────
9 8 7 1
```

2.	S E N D	9 5 6 7
	+ M O R E	+ 1 0 8 5
	M O N E Y	1 0 6 5 2

3. $\dfrac{T O P}{H A T} = H$ $\dfrac{4 6 8}{2 3 4} = 2$

4.	S U N	1 3 6
	+ F U N	+ 9 3 6
	S W I M	1 0 7 2

LOGICAL DEDUCTION

It has always been assumed that instruction in mathematics trained the mind and helped students learn to think. In reality, this translates to the ability to make proper logical deductions. Training in making logical deductions appears in formal geometry courses, and only rarely in other parts of the mathematics program. Successful problem solving depends upon the ability to draw conclusions from sets of data.

In Activities 4.10–4.12, we present a series of exercises designed to assist your students in obtaining some skill in drawing valid conclusions from a set of data. In addition, we present some problems whose solution depends upon logical deduction.

Activity 4.10

This activity presents some simple syllogisms. Have your students test the conclusion drawn from each pair of statements on Reproduction Page 78. Remember that a conclusion is true if it follows logically from the given statements, not necessarily from real life experiences.

Activity 4.11

Problem solving requires drawing proper conclusions from given data. Reproduction Pages 79 and 80 present the students with a collection of facts from which conclusions have been drawn. Have the students decide whether each conclusion is true, false, or cannot be determined from the given data.

Activity 4.12

This activity requires more sophisticated thought by the students than in the previous ones. It serves as a transition from the simple syllogisms in Activity 4.10 to the problems that will follow.

We lead the students to conclusions by having them examine separate statements and combinations of statements. The format on Reproduction Pages 81 and 82 represents the model we want the students to adopt.

Activity 4.13

Use the subskills from the previous three activities to solve the following problems.

> *Problem*   (Reproduction Page 83)
>
> Three cars are left in the Detroit Demolition Derby: a 1976 Ford, a bright red Cadillac with a dented fender, and a blue Lincoln with a vinyl roof. The drivers are Bill, Charley and Sue. Who is driving each car?
>
> 1. Sue drove into the Lincoln.
> 2. Sue said, "I'm going to get that Cadillac!"
> 3. Bill saw the Cadillac coming at him from the side.
> 4. Charley saw the Ford hit the Lincoln.

Discussion

From the first clue, students should reason that Sue cannot be driving the Lincoln. From the second clue, Sue cannot be driving the Cadillac. If they put an "X" in the proper boxes in the matrix, this will leave only the Ford for Sue to drive. Similar reasoning will make Bill the driver of the Lincoln and Charley the driver of the Cadillac.

> *Problem*   (Reproduction Page 84)
>
> On the way home, George, Harry, Ina and Jan stopped at the Sweet Tooth Ice Cream Parlor. They ordered the following items: a double-dip chocolate ice-cream cone, a banana split, a strawberry milk shake, and a caramel sundae. Who had which one?
>
> 1. The boys are allergic to chocolate.
> 2. The caramel got stuck in George's braces.
> 3. Jan said, "I like bananas!"
> 4. Jan bought a chocolate ice-cream cone and a strawberry milk shake for Ina and herself.
> 5. Ina shared some of what she had ordered with Harry.

Discussion

Clue number 1 allows us to eliminate the boys from the chocolate ice-cream cone. Clue number 2 assigns the caramel sundae to George. Clues 4 and 5 together tell us that Ina had the strawberry milkshake, since she shared some of it with Harry who is allergic to chocolate. Clue number 3 is merely a distractor.

ORGANIZED LISTING

Another strategy often used in problem solving is organized listing. In many problems, you have to exhaust all of the possibilities. However, this process can be shortened by observing what is taking place as the list is being developed. In these cases, an answer appears prior to the completion of the list.

Activity 4.14

These problems will give your students practice in developing and analyzing organized lists.

Problem (Reproduction Page 85)

In Mr. Gepetto's Clock Shop, two cuckoo clocks were brought in for repairs. One clock has the cuckoo coming out every six minutes, while the other one has the cuckoo coming out every eight minutes. Both cuckoos come out at 12:00 noon. When will they both come out together again?

Discussion

The solution to this problem lies in an organized list. Two lists should be made showing the times at which the cuckoo appears on each clock:

Clock 1	Clock 2
12:00	12:00
12:06	12:08
12:12	12:16
12:18	12:24
12:24	

Examination of the lists reveals the answer to be 12:24.

Problem

In how many different ways can you make change for a quarter?

Discussion

Sometimes an organized list is best revealed in table form. This coin problem is one of these. Columns for each kind of coin should be set up, and all possibilities considered:

Dimes	Nickels	Pennies
2	1	0
2	0	5
1	3	0
1	2	5
1	1	10
1	0	15
0	5	0
0	4	5
0	3	10
0	2	15
0	1	20
0	0	25

Problem   (Reproduction Page 86)

A farmer has some ducks and cows in the field. He sends his two children, Nancy and Jeff, to count the number of animals. Jeff reports back that he counted 70 heads. Nancy counted 200 legs. How many of each kind were counted?

Discussion

A list should be made which considers all of the possibilities.

Number of cows	Number of ducks	Number of heads			Number of legs		
		Cows	Ducks	Total	Cows	Ducks	Total
70	0	70	0	70	280	0	280
60	10	60	10	70	240	20	260
50	20	50	20	70	200	40	240
40	30	40	30	70	160	60	220
30	40	30	40	70	120	80	200

Problem   (Reproduction Page 87)

Lisa bought 48 feet of fencing in order to make a rectangular garden. What dimensions should she use to obtain the largest area? (Consider only whole numbers of feet.)

Discussion

A drawing will simplify the problem:

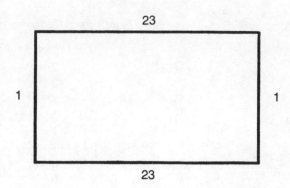

Figure 4.11

Since the area is the product of the length times the width, the critical number is the semi-perimeter, 24. The list will consist of the areas obtained for all possible perimeter combinations; i.e., 1 × 23, 2 × 22, 3 × 21, etc.

Length	Width	Area
23	1	23
22	2	44
21	3	63
⋮	⋮	⋮

Problem (Reproduction Page 88)

Mr. Chen wants to seed his front lawn. Grass seed is available in three pound boxes and five pound boxes. A three pound box costs $4.50, while a five pound box costs $6.58. Mr. Chen needs 17 pounds of the seed. How many of each size box should he purchase to get the best buy?

Discussion

In order to determine the best buy, a list must be made:

Number of 5-lb. Boxes	Cost at $6.58	Number of 3-lb. Boxes	Cost at $4.50	Total amount	Total cost
4	$26.32	0	0	20	$26.32
3	19.74	1	$ 4.50	18	24.24
2	13.16	3	13.50	19	26.66
1	6.58	4	18.00	17	24.58
0	0	6	27.00	18	27.00

Notice that in this case, the best buy is to purchase three 5-pound boxes and one 3-pound box, a total of 18 pounds, to get the 17 he needs.

WORKING BACKWARDS

Working backwards is a strategy that is successfully used when the outcome of a situation is known, and the initial conditions are required. A direct approach can also be used, but working backwards is more efficient. When we work backwards, the operations required by the original action will have to be reversed. That is, subtraction will replace addition, and division will replace multiplication.

Activity 4.15

The following problems illustrate the use of the working backwards strategy.

Problem

The local library fine schedule for overdue books is as follows:

> 10¢ per day for each of the first three days
> 7¢ per day thereafter

Sally paid a fine of $1.00. How many days was her book overdue?

Discussion

We know the final outcome was a $1.00 fine. Sally paid 30¢ for the first three days. This leaves 70¢ for the remainder of the fine. At 7¢ a day this is ten days. Her book was 13 days overdue.

If one attacked this problem directly, the order of operations would be to multiply 3 × 10¢ and *add* that to the product of 10 × 7¢. However, in the working backwards mode, we multiply 3 × 10¢, *subtract*, and then divide.

Problem (Reproduction Page 89)

Jimmy was trying a number trick on Sandy. He told her to pick a number, add 5 to it, multiply the sum by 3, then subtract 10 and double the result. Sandy's final answer was 28. What number did she start with?

Discussion

We begin with Sandy's answer, 28. Since she doubled the result we divide by 2 and get 14. She subtracted 10, so we add 10 (to get 24). Divide by 3 (8), subtract 5. Her starting number was 3.
Diagrammatically,

	Direct solution *(using algebraic symbols)*	*Working backwards solution*
Step 1	Let x = her number	
Step 2	add 5: x + 5	subtract 5: 3
Step 3	multiply by 3: 3(x + 5)	divide by 3: 8
Step 4	subtract 10: 3(x + 5) − 10	add 10: 24
Step 5	double the result: 2[3(x + 5) − 10]	halve the result: 14
Step 6	this equals 28: 2[3(x + 5) − 10] = 28	28

$$2[3x + 15 - 10] = 28$$
$$2[3x + 5] = 28$$
$$6x + 10 = 28$$
$$6x = 18$$
$$x = 3$$

Problem (Reproduction Page 90)

After receiving her weekly take-home pay, Marcy paid her roommate the $8 she owed for her share of the telephone bill. She then spent one-half of what was left on clothes, and then spent one-half of what was left on a concert ticket. She bought six stamps for 20¢ each, and had $12.10 left. What is her weekly take-home pay?

Discussion

Begin with the $12.10 that Marcy had left. Add the $1.20 she spent on stamps ($13.30). Since she spent *half* on a concert ticket, *multiply by two* ($26.60). She spent *half* on clothes; *multiply by two* ($53.20). She paid $8 for the telephone bill, so we *add* $8. Her take-home pay was $61.20.

Problem (Reproduction Page 91)

Alice, Beth and Carol decide to play a game of cards. They agree on the following procedure: when a player loses a game, she will double the amount of money that each of the other players already has. First Alice loses a hand, and doubles the amount of money that Beth and Carol each have. Then Beth loses a hand and doubles the amount of money that Alice and Carol each have. Then Carol loses a hand and doubles the amount of money that Alice and Beth each have. They then decide to quit, and find that each of them has exactly $8. How much did each of them start with?

Discussion

We represent the action with a list, while working backwards:

Alice	Beth	Carol	
$ 8	$ 8	$ 8	
4	4	16	
2	14	8	
13	7	4	(The amounts each started with)

CHAPTER 5

Solve

Once students have decided upon a strategy with which they hope to solve the problem, they reach the next step in which the problem is actually solved and the answer found. This step usually consists of applying a computational or algebraic skill to the facts assembled and organized in previous steps. This is a fairly routine procedure and its success depends upon the skills possessed by the students. If necessary, drill and practice in these manipulative operations should be provided from other sources. Of course the problems contained in this book also provide such practice.

However, certain problem-solving subskills required in this phase are not usually treated in traditional text material. They are (1) realizing there is insufficient data, and (2) dealing with multistage problems which involve recognizing hidden questions.

Activity 5.1

After the data has been organized, a strategy selected, and an arithmetic procedure initiated, the student may realize there is an insufficient amount of data. Something is missing! He or she must find this missing information, or the solution cannot be completed. Reproduction Page 92 presents a series of problems with missing information. Each problem is followed by three statements, one of which is the necessary information. The students should determine which of these facts completes the problem. Reproduction Page 93 presents a series of problems, again with information missing. Here, however, no choices are presented. Rather, the students must decide what information they would need in order to complete the solution.

Activity 5.2

According to the research in problem solving, children have *much* more trouble with two-stage and multi-stage problems than with one-stage problems. In a multi-stage problem, the solver is required to obtain some preliminary information from the problem itself before proceeding on to the final answer. For instance in the following problem

> There are five cages in the science laboratory, and each cage has three white mice. If a mouse eats 15 grams of food each week, how many grams of food do the mice eat each week?

the question to be answered is "How many grams of food do the mice eat each week?" Since the amount eaten by each mouse is known, the preliminary information needed is how many mice there are in the laboratory. This is the "Hidden Question."

Multi-stage problems present greater difficulty to students because they require this intermediate step, and because most of their problem-solving experiences taken from classroom texts involve single-stage problems.

This activity contains a series of multi-stage problems. Reproduction Pages 94 and 95 present two-stage problems. Students have to find the Hidden Question, the preliminary information they will need to solve the problem. Reproduction Pages 96 and 97 provide practice in multi-stage problems in which the student must answer several Hidden Questions.

CHAPTER 6

Looking Back

Once the student has found the answer to the problem, the tendency on the part of both students and teacher is to feel that the problem has been solved and the problem-solving process completed. This is not true! In actuality, there is valuable consideration that should still be given to a problem. It is in this stage, Looking Back, that the teacher should encourage students to decide whether or not the answer really makes sense and whether or not they have really answered the given question. Looking Back enables us to complete the problem-solving cycle. The Looking Back process includes comparing the derived answer with an estimated answer, verifying that the derived answer indeed makes sense, and reviewing the process by which the answer was obtained.

COMPARING THE DERIVED ANSWER WITH AN ESTIMATED ANSWER

Estimation, for our purposes, falls into two general categories, computational and visual. By computational estimation we include such things as being able to estimate the results of an addition, subtraction, multiplication or division example, estimation of time, and of ratio (such as unit pricing). By visual estimation, we include such things as estimating lengths, weights, capacities and areas.

Activity 6.1

Computational estimation requires that the student replace the specific numbers with approximations that are easy to use. The idea of estimation is to get the proper order of the answer, not the exact answer. Students should replace the given numbers with estimations to the nearest whole unit being considered. Thus 4.8 is replaced by 5; 32 is replaced by 30; 687 is replaced by 700; 1,125 is replaced by 1,000. Reproduction Page 98 will give your students practice in replacing numbers with estimates.

Activity 6.2

Approximating numbers prepares the student to estimate computation, our primary purpose. Reproduction Pages 99 and 100 give some experiences for students to do by estimation. It is suggested that a calculator be used after the estimates have been made. However, if drill and practice are needed in computation, these problems will provide this practice.

Activity 6.3	Reproduction Page 101 provides practice in estimation in a concrete setting. Have the students estimate each subtotal and then the total. Finally, have them actually compute the cost of each list and compare it with their estimates. Again, a calculator can be used for the actual computations.

Activity 6.4	Students are now ready to practice their estimation skills in a variety of settings. Reproduction Page 102 presents them with a series of problems, each followed by three answers. Have them select the answer they feel is the best estimate. Reproduction Page 103 contains a series of problems. Have the students estimate each answer, and then solve the problem. Compare the results with their estimates and discuss them with the entire class.

Activity 6.5	This activity calls upon the students' general knowledge to determine which of the three choices makes the most sense. In several cases, more than one of the choices would be appropriate. Reproduction Page 104 will provide discussion material to broaden their basic knowledge and thought processes.

Activity 6.6	Reproduction Pages 105 and 106 contain problems with answers. On Reproduction Page 105, some of the answers are correct, but most of them are not. Students are directed to state whether the given answer makes sense. They then complete the problem to check their choice. In Reproduction Page 106, all of the given answers are wrong! The students are directed to find what caused the error.

We have two purposes for this pair of activities. Our major thrust is to help students develop the ability to "eyeball" a problem and arrive at a reasonable approximation to the correct answer. Secondly, the reproduction pages provide extra practice in problem solving. In particular, Reproduction Page 106 gives the student a chance to uncover errors often made in the computational phase of the problem-solving process.

CHAPTER 7

A Collection of Strategy Games

Much of the current research shows a strong connection between problem solving and strategy games. That is, people who are good problem solvers are usually good strategy game players, and people who are good at playing strategy games usually exhibit an intuitive knowledge of problem solving.

The process for developing a winning strategy in gaming is virtually identical to developing the process of problem solving. In this chapter, we provide a series of strategy games, each with complete instructions and a game board where appropriate. Specific instructions for their use follows.

When using strategy games as an instructional model, there is a series of basic questions that must be addressed. Discuss these questions with the students.

- What are the rules?
- What constitutes a "win" or a "loss"?
- What is a "move"?
- Is it advantageous to go first?
- What should be the opening move?

When students have won a game several times, the entire class should stop and discuss what was done and what strategy was followed that produced the "win." If it was not just random play or luck, then the strategy of the game should emerge as the problem-solving process is followed.

Activity 7.1

TIC-TAC-TOE

The basic game of Tic-Tac-Toe is well known to most students. But how many of them have ever analyzed the game to develop a winning strategy? If the game is played correctly, it will usually result in a draw. However, we shall begin this chapter on strategy games with Tic-Tac-Toe, since students already know the basic rules of this two-person game.

(a) Variety Tic-Tac-Toe

Since students are already familiar with the rules and play of Tic-Tac-Toe, a simple change in the gameboard will produce what is in effect a "new" strategy game. Figure 7.1 shows some of the many possible game boards that can be used. (See Reproduction Pages 107–109.)

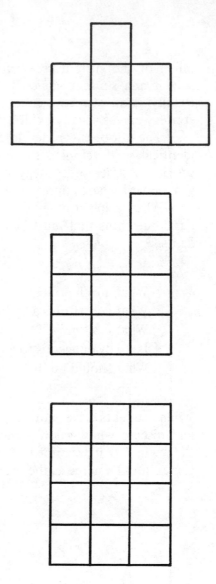

Figure 7.1 *Variety Tic-Tac-Toe Game Boards*

(b) 9-Cell Tic-Tac-Toe

Each of two players has three markers. They alternate turns putting their own markers down in any vacant cell on the 9-cell game board (Figure 7.2). When all six markers have been placed on the board, the players alternate turns moving any one of their own markers into an empty adjacent cell, either horizontally or vertically. The first player to get three of his or her own markers in a straight line in any direction (horizontally, vertically, or diagonally) is the winner. (See Reproduction Page 110.)

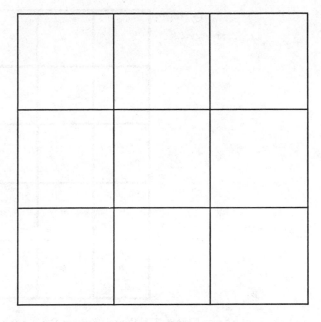

Figure 7.2 *9-Cell Tic-Tac-Toe Game Board*

(c) Line Tic-Tac-Toe

Fifteen dots are placed in a straight line. Two players alternate turns placing an "X" through any one dot anywhere on the line. The first player to mark off a dot so that there are three consecutive dots marked is the winner. The game can also be played so the first player to mark the third consecutive X in the row is the *loser*. (See Reproduction Page 111.)

(d) 5 × 5 Tic-Tac-Toe

This game is played on a game board consisting of 25 square cells in a 5 × 5 array, as shown in Figure 7.3. Each of two players has four distinctive markers. Players alternate turns placing their markers into any empty cell on the board. When all eight markers have been placed, they alternate turns moving any one of their own markers into any adjacent, vacant cell, either horizontally or vertically but not diagonally. To win, a player must get four markers in a row, horizontally, vertically or diagonally. A player also wins if he or she can get four markers into a two by two square. (See Reproduction Page 112.)

(e) Cross-'Em-Out Tic-Tac-Toe

Sixteen circles are placed in a 4 × 4 array as shown in Figure 7.4. Players alternate turns crossing out circles. Any number of circles may be crossed out in a turn, providing they are adjacent circles in a horizontal or vertical row

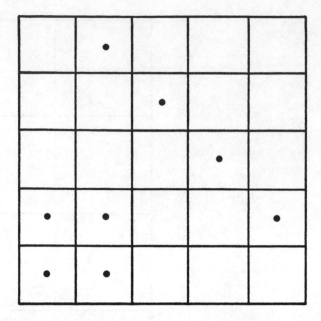

Figure 7.3 *Some Winning Positions on a 5 X 5 Tic-Tac-Toe Game Board*

with no spaces between. Thus, if a player removes circles 2 and 3, then circles 1 and 4 cannot be taken on any one turn. The player who crosses out the final circle is the winner. (Again, this game can be played so the player who is forced to cross out the final circle is the loser.) (See Reproduction Page 113.)

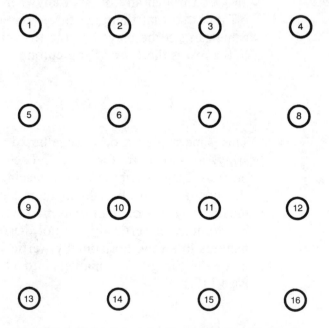

Figure 7.4 *Game Board for Cross-'Em-Out Tic-Tac-Toe*

(f) 13-Cell Tic-Tac-Toe

The board for this game contains 13 cells connected by a series of straight lines. Each of the two players has three distinctive markers. The players al-

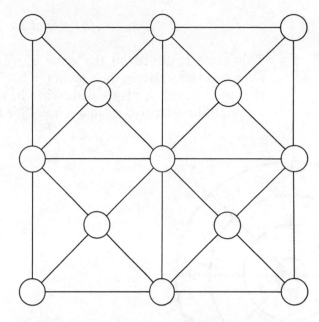

Figure 7.5 *13-Cell Tic-Tac-Toe Game Board*

ternate turns placing one of their markers in any empty cell on the game board. (The center cell cannot be used until all six markers have been placed on the board.) After all the pieces are placed, players take turns moving any one of their own pieces along a line to the next vacant, adjacent cell. The winner is the first player to have his or her three pieces in a row, vertically, horizontally, or diagonally. (See Reproduction Page 114.)

(g) Triangular Tic-Tac-Toe

This version of Tic-Tac-Toe utilizes the rules for the basic game. That is, the students alternate turns placing either an "X" or an "O" into any empty cell in an attempt to get three pieces in a straight line. The unusual shape of the game board provides an opportunity for careful analysis of the game. (See Reproduction Page 115.)

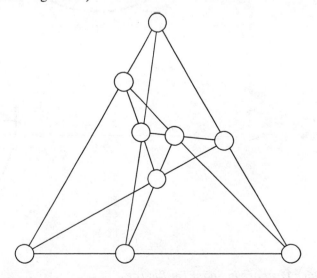

Figure 7.6 *Triangular Tic-Tac-Toe Game Board*

(h) Spiral Tic-Tac-Toe

This game is played on the game board shown in Figure 7.7. Two players alternate turns placing their mark (an "X" or an "O") in any empty space on the game board. A player wins when he or she has four in a "row," either in a straight line, a circle, or in a spiral. (See Reproduction Page 116.)

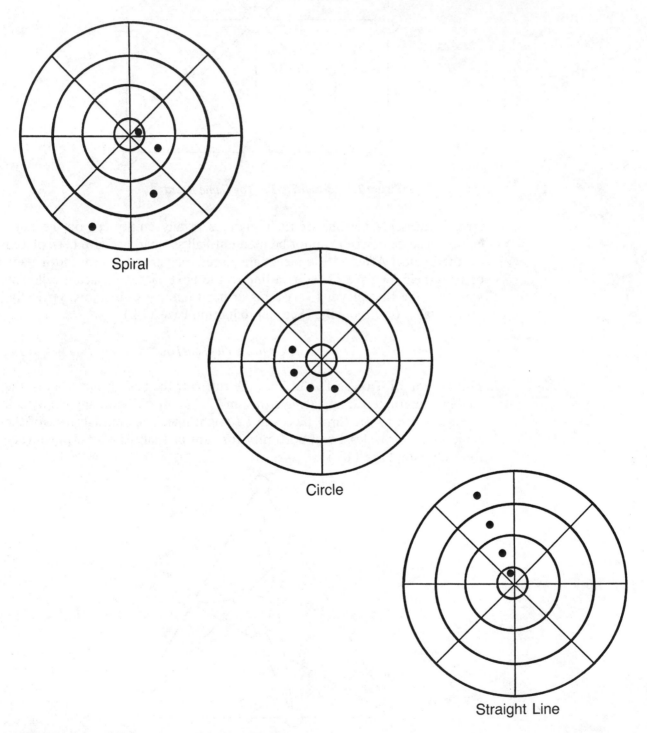

Figure 7.7 *Winning Positions in Spiral Tic-Tac-Toe*

The strategy games in this section are all related in some way to checkers. That is, they may be played on a standard 8 X 8 checkerboard, or they may follow the basic rules of checkers but use a different board. Again, we remind you to encourage your students to reflect on their moves and to attempt to develop a plan for their play. Their strategies should be discussed whether they lead to a win or not. It is this plan development that aids the students with problem solving.

(a) Makesquare

This game is played on the standard 8 X 8 checkerboard. One player uses up to 32 checkers (or other markers) of one color; the opponent uses up to 32 checkers of another color. Players alternate turns placing one of their own markers in any empty square. The first player whose four checkers form the vertices of a square is the loser. (See Reproduction Page 117.)

(b) Sheep and Wolves

This is a game of entrapment played on the 8 X 8 checkerboard. That is, the sheep try to trap the wolf so that he cannot move. The player who is the "sheep" places four checkers of one color on the four black squares at one end of the board. The "wolf," a checker of another color, is placed on any black square at the opposite end of the board. Players alternate turns. The sheep can move one square diagonally along the black squares as in checkers. They cannot move backwards. The wolf may move backwards or forwards, also on the diagonal, one square at a time. There is no jumping or capturing. The sheep wins when they "pen" the wolf so that he cannot move. The wolf wins when he gets into a section of the board where he cannot be reached by the sheep. (See Reproduction Page 117.)

(c) Triangular Checkers

Here is another situation in which the radically different appearance of the game board causes the students to develop an entirely new strategy. The game is played according to the rules of checkers. Each player places his or her checkers in the nine cells as indicated in Figure 7.8. The center cell is left open. Players alternate turns moving one of their own pieces along any line to any adjacent, unoccupied cell. If the adjacent cell is occupied by an opponent's piece but the next cell in that line is vacant, the player may jump over the piece to the vacant cell, removing the jumped piece from the board. Multiple jumps on the same move are permitted. Pieces may be moved in any direction. The winner is the player who captures all of the opponent's playing pieces. If a player cannot move because all of his or her pieces are blocked, that player is the loser. (See Reproduction Page 118.)

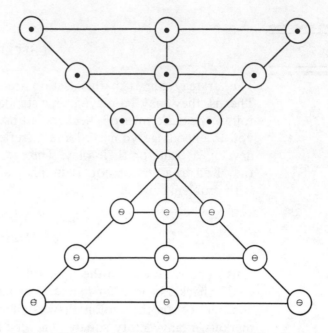

Figure 7.8 *Starting Position for Triangular Checkers*

(d) Circular Checkers

This is another version of checkers for two players. The pieces are placed on the gameboard as shown in Figure 7.9. The center cell is left open. Players alternate turns moving along any line (straight or curved) to any adjacent, vacant cell. If the cell is occupied by an opponent's piece but the next cell along that line is vacant, the player may jump over the opponent's piece and remove it from the board. Multiple jumps on the same move are permitted. The winner is the player who captures all of his or her opponent's

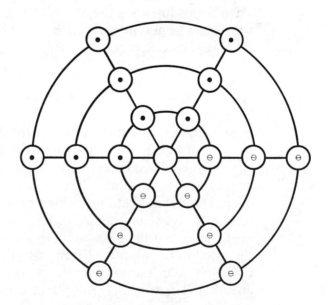

Figure 7.9 *Starting Position for Circular Checkers*

pieces. If a player is blocked and cannot move, that player is the loser of the game. (See Reproduction Page 119.)

(e) 5 × 5 Checkers

This game is played on a 5 × 5 square checkerboard with 25 markers. Players alternate turns placing markers in vacant boxes on the board. A player may place as many markers as he or she wishes, as long as the markers are all placed in the same horizontal or vertical line during that turn. The winner is the player who puts down the 25th and final marker. (See Reproduction Page 120.)

Activity 7.3

MISCELLANEOUS STRATEGY GAMES

(a) Split

This is a game for two players. Play begins with a pile of 32 matchsticks or checkers in the center of the table. Each player in his or her turn must separate *any* existing pile into *two unequal-sized piles.* Thus a pile of four chips must be separated into piles of three and one, but it cannot be separated into piles of two and two. Similarly, a pile of two chips can never be separated. The first player who cannot make a move is the loser.

(b) Making Bridges

The game of Making Bridges is a game for two players. The objective is to be the first player to make a continuous path from one side of the game board to the other. One player connects the Os, the other connects the Xs. Players alternate turns connecting any two of their own marks with a horizontal or vertical line. A line may not cross any other line. The first player to reach the opposite side of the board with a continous path is the winner. (See Reproduction Page 121.)

(c) Two-Way Traffic

In this game for two players, each player has two chips or other markers which are placed on the two tracks as shown in Figure 7.10. Players alternate turns moving either of their own pieces up or down, following these two rules:

1. The piece being moved does not leave the track it is on.
2. The piece being moved does not pass over the opponent's piece in that same row.

The first player who cannot move either piece is the loser. (See Reproduction Page 122.)

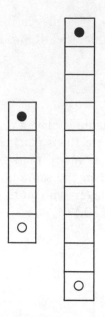

Figure 7.10 *Starting Position for Two-Way Traffic*

(d) Wandering Rooks

Two players each have five chips or other markers placed on the 8 X 5 rectangular board as shown in Figure 7.11. The players, in turn, move any one of their own chips as far as desired up or down a row following these two rules:

1. The piece being moved does not leave the row it is in.
2. The piece being moved does not pass over the opponent's piece in that same row.

The first player who cannot move any of his or her pieces is the loser. (See Reproduction Page 123.)

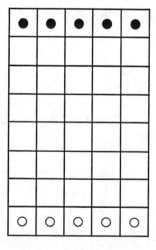

Figure 7.11 *Starting Position for Wandering Rooks*

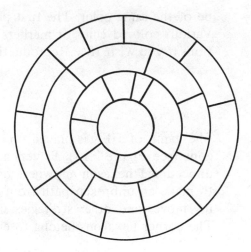

Figure 7.12 *A Typical Arrangement for the Four-Color Game*

(e) The Four-Color Game

This game can be played by two, three or four players. The game board is divided into various numbers of regions. One example is shown in Figure 7.12. Each player, in turn, colors any region of his or her choice with an identifiable color. However, the regions adjacent to each other *may not*

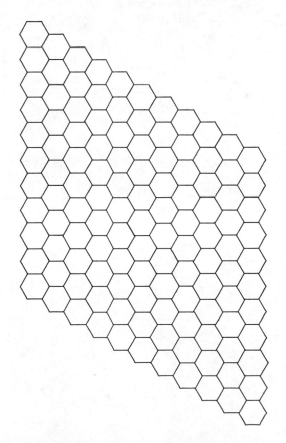

Figure 7.13 *A HEX Game Board*

be of the same color. The first player who cannot make a move is the loser. Various colored chips or markers can be used instead of coloring in the sections if you wish. (See Reproduction Page 124.)

(f) HEX

The game of HEX is played on a diamond-shaped board made up of hexagons (see Figure 7.13). Players alternate turns placing an X or an O in any unoccupied hexagon anywhere on the board. The winner is the first player to make an unbroken path from one side of the board to the other. Blocking moves and other strategies should be developed as the game proceeds. The corner hexagons belong to either player. (See Reproduction Page 125.)

CHAPTER **8**

A Collection of
Non-Routine Problems

Problems 1–15 are particularly applicable to the elementary school student. Problems 16–35 are particularly applicable to the junior high school student. Problems 36–50 are particularly applicable to the senior high school student. Problems marked with an asterisk are easily adaptable to other levels.

Problem 1 (Reproduction Page 126)

Circle two numbers whose quotient is 8.

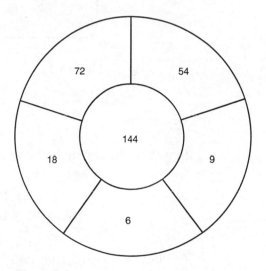

Figure 8.1

Discussion

Guess and test. The problem has two answers.

Problem 2 (Reproduction Page 127)

Find all of the two digit numbers for which the sum of the two digits is 10.

Discussion

Make a list, and notice the pattern. The list *is* the answer.

19, 28, 37, 46, 55, 64, 73, 82, 91

Problem 3 (Reproduction Page 128)

A spider wishes to crawl from point H to point B (see Figure 8-2). How many different "trips" can he crawl, if each trip is exactly three edges long?

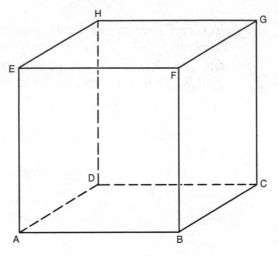

Figure 8.2

Discussion

Simulate the trip and make a record of the paths.

H-E-F-B	H-G-C-B	H-D-A-B
H-E-A-B	H-G-F-B	H-D-C-B

Problem 4 (Reproduction Page 129)

I have five coins: quarters, nickels, and dimes. The total value of the coins is 50¢. How many of each coin do I have?

Discussion

Make an exhaustive list.

Quarters	Dimes	Nickels	Total	Number of coins
2	0	0	50¢	2
1	2	1	50¢	4
1	1	3	50¢	5
0	5	0	50¢	5

Since all coins were represented, only the third row is a correct answer.

Problem 5 (Reproduction Page 129)

The six students in Mr. Charne's biology class were arranged numerically around a hexagonal table. What number student was opposite number 4?

Discussion

Draw a diagram.

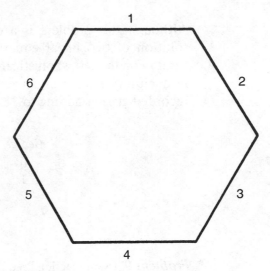

Figure 8.3

Problem 6 (Reproduction Page 130)

Jim is in line at the bridge waiting to pay his toll. He counts four cars in front of him and six cars behind him. How many cars are there in line at the bridge?

Discussion

Act it out, or draw a diagram using Xs to represent the cars in line. Don't forget to count Jim's car, too.

Problem 7 (Reproduction Page 130)

The listed price for *Sports Magazine* is $1.25 a copy. You pay $16.56 for a 24-issue subscription. How much do you save by buying the subscription?

Discussion

This is an example of a two-stage problem. Students first find the total cost of 24 copies at the per issue rate, then subtract the subscription price from this total.

Problem 8 (Reproduction Page 131)

Last Saturday, George and his friend Mike went to a big-league baseball game. After the game, they went to the locker room to collect autographs of their favorite players. Together they collected eighteen autographs, but Mike collected four more than George. How many did George collect?

Discussion

Although this problem is a classic example of the simultaneous solution of two linear equations, it provides an excellent opportunity for the less sophisticated student to practice guess and test in conjunction with organized listing. A series of carefully chosen recorded guesses adding to 18 leads to the numbers 11 and 7.

George	Mike	Total
0	18	18
1	17	18
2	16	18
⋮	⋮	⋮

* *Problem 9* (Reproduction Page 131)

Norene set her wristwatch when she left for school at exactly 7:30 a.m. on Monday. At 1:30 p.m. on Monday, she noticed that her watch had lost 4 minutes. At this same rate, how many minutes will the watch lose by the time Norene resets it when she leaves for school at 7:30 a.m. on Tuesday?

Discussion

Although this problem can be solved by many students by counting, since clock arithmetic is in base 12, others may need a picture of a clock to illustrate the situation. From the drawing, students should see that the elapsed time between 7:30 a.m. and 1:30 p.m. is 6 hours. Thus,

$$\frac{4 \text{ minutes}}{? \text{ minutes}} = \frac{6 \text{ hours}}{24 \text{ hours}}$$

Problem 10 (Reproduction Page 132)

The faces of a cube are numbered with consecutive numbers. Three of the numbers are shown. What is the sum of the numbers on all the faces of the cube?

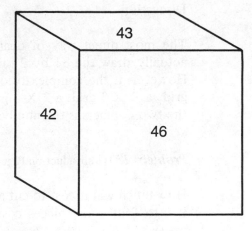

Figure 8.4

Discussion

A knowledge of arithmetic is all that is necessary to solve this problem. Since a cube has six faces, we need six consecutive numbers. There is more than one solution to this problem. That is, the 42 can be the lowest number (and the sum would be 42 + 43 + 44 + 45 + 46 + 47 = 267), or the highest number might be 46 (and the sum would then be 41 + 42 + 43 + 44 + 45 + 46 = 261).

Problem 11 (Reproduction Page 133)

Laura jogs seven blocks the first day of her training program. She increases her distance by two blocks each day. On the last day, she jogs 25 blocks. How many days was she in training?

Discussion

Make a list.

Day	Number of blocks
1	7
2	9
3	11
⋮	⋮

Problem 12 (Reproduction Page 133)

The town of Graphville has intersections formed by 27 avenues that run north-sorth, and 31 streets that run east-west. If we plan one traffic light at each intersection, how many traffic lights do we need?

Discussion

The most direct way of dealing with this problem would be to actually draw the 31 by 27 line grid and count the intersections. However, if the complexity of the numbers is reduced to a 2 × 2 grid, a 2 × 3 grid, a 2 × 4 grid, etc., we see that the product of the two numbers is the number of intersections.

Problem 13 (Reproduction Page 134)

How much will it cost to cut a log into eight equal pieces if cutting it into four equal pieces costs 60¢? There is no stacking of the pieces.

Discussion

Make a drawing of the log. It is easy to see that cutting the log into four pieces requires only three cuts. Thus each cut costs 20¢. To cut the log into eight equal pieces, we need only seven cuts at 20¢ each, or $1.40.

Problem 14 (Reproduction Page 134)

My license tag is a three-digit number. The product of the digits is 216, their sum is 19, and the numbers appear in ascending order. Find my license plate number.

Discussion

Make a list of all the number triples whose product is 216 and which are single digits. There are only three such triples:

$$3, 8, 9$$
$$4, 6, 9$$
$$6, 6, 6$$

Of these, only 4, 6, and 9 satisfy the conditions.
    This problem also provides a considerable amount of drill and practice in factors, multiplication and division.

* Problem 15 (Reproduction Page 135)

Mr. Lopez' class collected $5.29 for a class gift. Each student contributed the same amount, and each paid with the same five coins. How many dimes were collected?

Discussion

Guess and test will help provide the solution to this problem. If we could find the number of students involved, we would be able to find out how much each paid. Trying successive numbers to find a divisor of $5.29 leads us to 23 students who paid 23¢ each. The only way to pay 23¢ with five coins is to pay two dimes and three pennies. Thus 46 dimes were collected.

Problem 16 (Reproduction Page 136)

A fancy bottle of perfume costs $25. The bottle can be purchased by collectors without the perfume. When purchased this way the bottle costs $15 less than the perfume. How much does the bottle cost alone?

Discussion

Guess and test provides an alternative to the algebraic solution. Since the total for the bottle and perfume is $25, one could guess $1 for the bottle which leaves $24 for the perfume. Listing the guesses is an important skill.

Bottle	Perfume	Total
1	24	25
2	23	25
⋮	⋮	⋮
5	20	25

Problem 17 (Reproduction Page 136)

In a recent sale at the local stationery store, the following sign appeared:

```
┌──────────────────────────────┐
│        ERASERS  5¢            │
│        PENCILS  7¢            │
│   LIMIT: 3 OF EACH TO A       │
│        CUSTOMER               │
└──────────────────────────────┘
```

If you had 20¢ to spend, what different combinations of pencils and erasers could you buy?

Discussion

An organized list is the strategy to adopt.

Pencils	Cost	Erasers	Cost	Total cost
3	21¢	0	0¢	not possible
3	21¢	1	5¢	not possible
3	21¢	2	10¢	not possible
3	21¢	3	15¢	not possible
2	14¢	0	0¢	14¢
2	14¢	1	5¢	19¢
2	14¢	2	10¢	not possible
2	14¢	3	15¢	not possible
1	7¢	0	0¢	7¢
⋮	⋮	⋮	⋮	⋮

Problem 18 (Reproduction Page 137)

The Kudin family is putting a fence around their garden which is in the shape of a square. If there will be seven posts on each side of the square, how many posts are there altogether?

Discussion

Study the drawing in Figure 8.5. Note that there are four corner posts that are on more than one side of the square. Thus these must be discounted when we take the sum of the posts. The correct answer would be 28 − 4 or 24 posts.

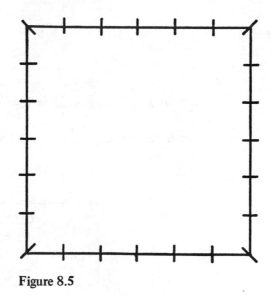

Figure 8.5

Problem 19 (Reproduction Page 137)

Replace each of the question marks with the same number so that the fractions will be equivalent. What is the number?

$$\frac{2}{?} = \frac{?}{32}$$

Discussion

Algebraically, the question marks can be replaced by variables and the equation $x^2 = 64$ is obtained because the product of the means equals the product of the extremes. An alternate strategy would be to guess and test.

Problem 20 (Reproduction Page 138)

The Iowa Falcons and the Indiana Bombers set a new semi-pro league record last week when they scored 362 points between them in one game. If the Falcons lost by 14 points, how many points did the Bombers score?

Discussion

Guess and test along with an organized list or table would seem appropriate:

Bombers	Falcons	Total	Difference
200	162	362	38
190	172	362	18
188	174	362	14

Problem 21 (Reproduction Page 138)

To help earn spending money in school, Ruth bought some Indian Head pennies at 6 for $10, and then sold them at 4 for $10. She made a total of $50 profit. How many pennies did she buy and sell?

Discussion

Have the students make a list. Note that the left hand column must be the common multiples of 4 and 6.

Number bought	Cost	Selling price	Profit
12	$ 20	$ 30	$10
24	40	60	20
36	60	90	30
48	80	120	40
60	100	150	50

She bought and sold 60 Indian Head pennies.

Problem 22 (Reproduction Page 139)

Fill in Figure 8.6 with the digits from 1 through 8 so that no two consecutive numbers have a point or a side in common.

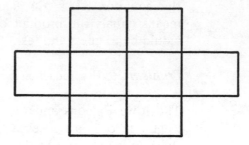

Figure 8.6

Discussion

By guess and test we arrive at the solution shown in Figure 8.7.

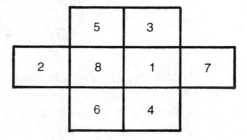

Figure 8.7

* Problem 23 (Reproduction Page 139)

Jason computed his average for five tests in his math class, and found he had a 76. What must he score on the final two tests in order to raise his average to 80?

Discussion

An average of 76 for five tests means that Jason had a total of 5 × 76 or 380 points. In order to have a final average of 80 for seven tests he must accumulate a total of 7 × 80 or 560 points. Thus he must score 180 points on the next two tests.

A man takes a 5,000 mile trip in his car. He rotates his tires (4 on the car and 1 spare) so that at the end of the trip each tire had been used for the same number of miles. How many miles were drived on each tire?

Discussion

Since four tires are always in use, we are really talking about 4 X 5,000 miles or 20,000 miles of tire use. Thus, 20,000 divided by five tires means each was used for a total of 4,000 miles.

Problem 25 (Reproduction Page 140)

A 42 ounce can of Fruity Drink contains 7 ounces of pure fruit juice, and the remainder is water and additives. If Georgette drinks 6 ounces of the fruit drink, how much pure fruit juice does she consume?

Discussion

This problem merely illustrates and uses the arithmetic concept of proportions.

Problem 26 (Reproduction Page 141)

There are four numbers less than 1,000 that are both perfect squares and also perfect cubes. Find them.

Discussion

An exhaustive listing or the guess and test strategy may be used.
Make two lists, one of the perfect squares and one of the perfect cubes. Then find the elements common to these two lists.

Cubes	Squares
0	0
1	1
8	4
27	9
64	16
125	25
216	36
⋮	⋮

Problem 27 (Reproduction Page 141)

Linda is playing "Guess My Number" with her classmates. See if you can find her number from the following clues:

(a) her number is a multiple of 5

(b) it is less than 200

(c) it is divisible by 3

(d) its ten's digit equals the sum of its other two digits.

Discussion

This problem can be dealt with by the use of an exhaustive list of possible solutions. Clue (b) places an upper limit on the number, while clue (d) places a lower limit. Thus the number lies between 100 and 200. Clues (a) and (c) state that the number is a multiple of 15, since 3 and 5 are primes.

The four clues when put together lead to the list 105, 120, 135, 150, 165, 180, and 195. Clue (d) specifically identifies the number as 165.

Problem 28 (Reproduction Page 142)

A stadium holds 100,000 people. Ushers estimated that 3 males came in for every 2 females. How many males and how many females were in the stadium?

Discussion

Simplify and extend.

Assume 5 people and that these are 3 males and 2 females. If there were 10 people, these would be 6 males and 4 females. 100,000 is 10,000 × 10, so there would be

$$6 \times 10,000 \text{ males and}$$
$$4 \times 10,000 \text{ females}$$

or 60,000 males and 40,000 females.

Problem 29 (Reproduction Page 142)

When Sue places marbles in boxes by 2s, she has one left over. If she puts them in the boxes by 3s, she has one left over. And, if she puts them in by 5s, she still has one left over. What is the smallest number of marbles she can use to do this?

Discussion

Three lists of numbers which give remainders of 1 when divided by 2, 3, and 5 respectively should be made. Find the smallest number that appears on all three lists.

	By 2s	By 3s	By 5s
	3	4	5
	5	7	11
	7	10	16
	9	13	21
	11	16	26
	13	19	(31)
	15	22	36
	17	25	41
	19	28	
	21	(31)	
	23	34	
	25		
	27		
	29		
	(31)		

Problem 30 (Reproduction Page 143)

Find a number that when multiplied by 81 or divided into 6,561 gives the same answer.

Discussion

Guess and test.

Try 10. $81 \times 10 = 810$
$6561 \div 10 = 656.1$ No good

Try 9. $81 \times 9 = 729$
$6561 \div 9 = 729$

Problem 31 (Reproduction Page 143)

A neighborhood pet shop sells only dogs and birds. One morning they count a total of 10 heads and 34 legs. How many dogs and how many birds do they have?

Discussion

Make a table showing the possible combinations. The required answer will be evident.

BIRDS	DOGS	TOTAL HEADS	TOTAL LEGS	
10	0	10	20	(too few legs)
5	5	10	30	(too few legs)
4	6	10	32	(still too few)
3	7	10	34	(just right!)

Problem 32 (Reproduction Page 144)

It costs a dime to cut and weld a chain-link. What is the minimum number of cuts needed to make a single chain from seven individual links?

Discussion

Make a series of drawings as shown in Figure 8.8.

(a)

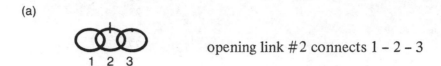

opening link #2 connects 1 – 2 – 3

(b)

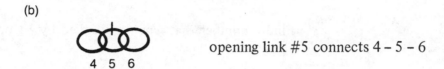

opening link #5 connects 4 – 5 – 6

(c)

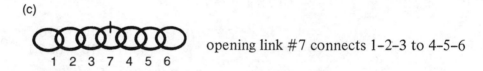

opening link #7 connects 1–2–3 to 4–5–6

Figure 8.8

Problem 33 (Reproduction Page 144)

Jeff has a record collection. If he stacks them in piles of seven, he has no records left over. But, when he puts them into piles of 2, 3, or 4, he always has one record left over. What is the minimum number of records Jeff has in his collection?

Discussion

This problem can be solved by using guess and test along with an understanding of the fundamentals of simple division, i.e., what is the meaning of a remainder.

The first statement says the number of records in the collection is a multiple of 7. Thus all that is needed is to list these multiples and find the first one that leaves a remainder of one when divided by 2, 3, and 4.

7, 14, 21, 28, 35, 42, ⑭, 56, 63, 70

In the outer reaches of space there are eleven relay stations for the Intergalactic Space Ship Line. There are space ship routes between the relay stations as shown on the map in Figure 8.9.

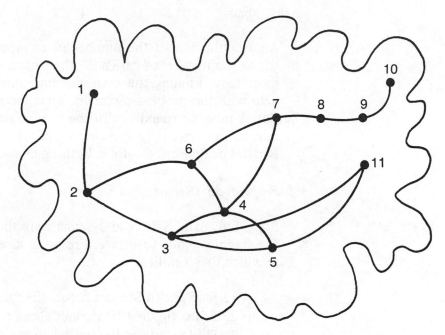

Figure 8.9

Eleven people have been engaged as communications operators, one for each station. The people are Alex, Barbara, Cindy, Donna, Elvis, Frances, Gloria, Hal, Irene, Johnny and Karl. The two people in the stations with connecting routes will be talking to each other a great deal, to discuss the space ships that fly from station to station. It would be helpful if these people were friendly to each other. Here are the pairs of people who are friends:

Alex-Barbara	Hal-Frances	Irene-Karl	Johnny-Irene
Gloria-Johnny	Gloria-Irene	Donna-Elvis	Johnny-Cindy
Donna-Irene	Alex-Gloria	Karl-Elvis	Donna-Karl
Cindy-Hal	Alex-Donna		

Place the eleven people in the eleven stations so that the people in connecting stations are friends.

Discussion

Make a table and use logical thought.

	A	B	C	D	E	F	G	H	I	J	K
People	B	A	H	I	D	H	J	F	K	I	E
to whom	G		J	E	K		I	C	D	C	I
they	D			K			A		G	G	D
talk				A					J		
Total	3	1	2	4	2	1	3	2	4	3	3

An examination of the number of connections for each station shows the number of "friends" the person assigned to the station must have. Finding the corresponding numbers in the table will help with the people-assignment. Thus the person assigned to station 1 must be friendly with the one assigned to station 2. Since that is his or her only speaking friend, the spot must go to either Barbara or Frances. Continue in this manner.

* **Problem 35** (Reproduction Page 146)

Stan, Stu, Sam, Shirley and Selma were the first five finishers of the seventeen-mile road race. From the given clues, give the order in which they finished.

 1. Stan passed Stu just before the finish line.
 2. Selma finished 10 seconds ahead of Stan.
 3. Shirley crossed the finish line in a dead heat with Stu.
 4. Sam was fifth at the finish.

Discussion

This is a familiar type of logic problem that can be solved by translating each clue to a line figure:

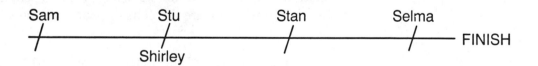

Clue 1 places Stan ahead of Stu
Clue 2 places Selma ahead of Stan
Clue 3 places Shirley at the same point as Stu
Clue 4 places Sam last

Problem 36 (Reproduction Page 147)

How many arrows will it take to hit the target and score exactly 100?

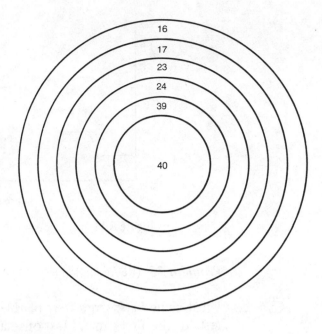

Figure 8.10

Discussion

By guess and test, we find one solution to be $4 \times 17 + 2 \times 16$ or six arrows.

* Problem 37 (Reproduction Page 148)

Current postal rates for a first class letter are 20¢ for the first ounce or fraction thereof, and 17¢ for each additional ounce or fraction.

(a) How much would it cost to mail a first class letter that weighs 3½ ounces?

(b) A first class letter was mailed and cost $1.05 in postage. What did it weigh?

Discussion

Part (a) of the problem is solved by considering the weight of the letter as two parts: the first ounce (20¢) and the remaining 2½ ounces which are counted as 3 ounces. The three ounces cost 3×17¢ or 51¢, plus the first ounce at 20¢ for a total cost of 71¢.

Part (b) presents the student with a different kind of problem, that is, one for which there is no unique answer but rather a range of weights. It is best done by constructing a graph as shown in Figure 8.11 from which the answer is easily found. The graph is a step function which may be a new experience for most students.

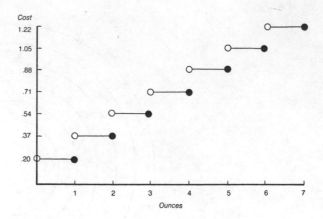

Figure 8.11

Problem 38 (Reproduction Page 149)

I just came back from four marble games. I have only 21 marbles left. In the first game, I lost one-half of my marbles. In the second game I won 12 times what I had. In the third game, I won 9 more marbles. But in the fourth game, the game was a draw and no marbles were exchanged. I forgot how many marbles I began with. Can you tell me how many I had when I started?

Discussion

Two methods seem likely. First, let's work backwards.

> I have 21.
> I won 9, so I must have had 12.
> I won 12 times what I had, so I had 1.
> I lost half, so I started with 2.

Second, let's start with "*x*" marbles and proceed:

> x
> $x/2$
> $6x$
> $6x + 9$
> $6x + 9 = 21$
> $\quad 6x = 12$
> $\quad\ x = \ 2$

Students can also guess at a starting number and work from there.

Problem 39 (Reproduction Page 150)

Steve is responsible for keeping the fish tanks in the Seaside Aquarium Shop filled with water. One of their 50-gallon tanks has a small leak, and, along with evaporation, loses 2 gallons of water each day. Every three days, Steve adds 5 gallons of water to the tank, and on the 30th day he fills it. How much water will he have to add on the 30th day to fill the tank?

Discussion

There are several solutions to this interesting problem. The first is to notice that there is a net loss of one gallon every three days, which means a loss of ten gallons during the thirty day interval. Thus Steve must add 10 gallons on the thirtieth day.

A more interesting solution is achieved by drawing a graph of the situation, which turns out to be a sawtooth graph as shown in Figure 8.12.

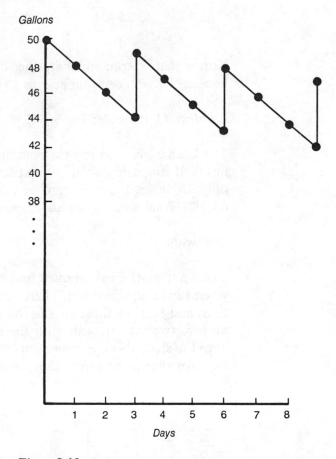

Figure 8.12

Problem 40 (Reproduction Page 151)

The numbers on the uniforms of the Granville Baseball Team all consist of two digits. Two friends on the team are also amateur mathematicians. They select their numbers so the square of the sum of their numbers is the same as the four-digit number formed by their uniforms when they stand side by side. What are the numbers on their uniforms?

Discussion

Exhaustive listing with the use of a calculator provides a solution. The problem tells us that the square of the sum of the two numbers is a four-digit number. Thus n^2 lies between 1,000 and 10,000. Use a calculator to identify all the perfect squares between the limits and see which satisfy the condition.

There are only three possible answers:

$$98\ 01 = (99)^2 = (98 + 01)^2 \longrightarrow 98\ 01$$
$$30\ 25 = (55)^2 = (30 + 25)^2 \longrightarrow 30\ 25$$
$$20\ 25 = (45)^2 = (20 + 25)^2 \longrightarrow 20\ 25$$

Notice that we can eliminate the first possible answer (98 and 01) because 01 would not appear as a two-digit number on a uniform.

Problem 41 (Reproduction Page 152)

The license plate on my car contains five different digits. My son installed it upside down, yet it still shows a five-digit number. The only thing is, the new number exceeds the original number by 63,783. What was the original license number?

Discussion

Guess and test! First we must find out what numerals are readable when turned upside down. There are only five such numerals: 0, 1, 6, 8, and 9. Thus these are the five digits in the license plate. Now prepare two sets of cards with the numerals 0, 1, 6, 8 and 9, and have the students experiment until they find the answer.

An alternative approach is to examine the subtraction process to see what materials satisfy the conditions:

The only ways in which a 3 can be obtained in the units position would be to subtract 6 from 9 or 8 from 1, as shown in the drawing above. However, look what happens when the license plate is installed upside down

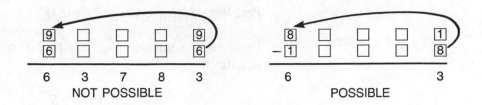

6   3   7   8   3   6   3
NOT POSSIBLE   POSSIBLE

Further guessing and testing concludes that the original license plate number was 16908.

Problem 42 (Reproduction Page 153)

Four couples play bridge every month. The wives' names are Gladys, Hariett, Susan and Bonnie. The husbands' names are Marv, Allan, Steve and Herb (but not in that order). Who is married to whom?

(a) Marv is Susan's brother.
(b) Susan and Herb were engaged, but broke up when Herb met his present wife.
(c) Bonnie has two brothers, but her husband is an only child.
(d) Gladys is married to Steve.

Discussion

Draw a matrix as shown:

	Gladys	Hariett	Susan	Bonnie
Marv			✕	
Allan				
Steve				
Herb			✕	

From the clues, cross out the blocks that cannot exist:

Clue 1 says that Susan and Marv are brother and sister, and are not a couple. Put an X in that block.
Clue 2 says that Susan and Herb are not a couple.

Continue in this fashion.

Problem 43 (Reproduction Page 154)

How many solutions can you find for R and S that satisfy the equation?

$$\frac{R}{S} + \frac{S}{R} = 2$$

Discussion

A straightforward solution is undertaken by solving the equation for R in terms of S as follows:

$$\frac{R}{S} + \frac{S}{R} = 2$$

$$\frac{R^2 + S^2}{RS} = 2$$

$$R^2 + S^2 = 2RS$$

$$R^2 + S^2 - 2RS = 0$$

$$(R - S)^2 = 0$$

$$R = S$$

An alternate solution for a student who has not studied algebra would be to analyze the statement $\frac{R}{S} + \frac{S}{R} = 2$ and guess at an answer. Since the two expressions add to two, it is fairly obvious that each should be 1 which means $R = S$.

Problem 44 (Reproduction Page 154)

Find the smallest perfect square of three digits such that the sum of these digits is not a perfect square.

Discussion

An organized list would be helpful. Since the perfect square is to contain three digits, the number itself must lie between 10 and 31 inclusive.

$10^2 = 100$ the sum of the digits is 1 which is
                   a perfect square
$11^2 = 121$ the sum of the digits is 4 which is
                   a perfect square
$12^2 = 144$ the sum of the digits is 9 which is
                   a perfect square

$\vdots$ $\vdots$

Continuing this list reveals that 256 (the square of 16) is the required number.

* **Problem 45** (Reproduction Page 155)

How many triangles are there in Figure 8.13?

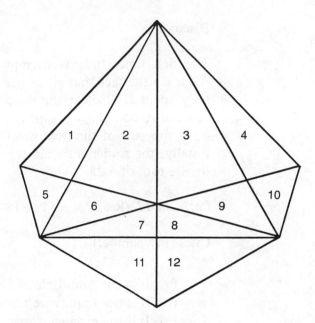

Figure 8.13

Discussion

An organized list would seem appropriate:

One region	Two regions	Three regions	Four regions	Six regions
1	1, 2	2, 3, 6	1, 2, 3, 9	2, 3, 6, 7, 8, 9
2	1, 5	2, 3, 9	2, 3, 4, 6	
3	2, 6	2, 6, 7	2, 6, 7, 11	
4	3, 4	3, 8, 9	3, 8, 9, 12	
5	3, 9	6, 7, 8	5, 6, 7, 8	
6	4, 10	7, 8, 9	7, 8, 9, 10	
7	5, 6			
8	7, 8			
9	7, 11			
10	8, 12			
11	9, 10			
12	11, 12			

Thus there are 37 different triangles in the diagram.

Problem 46 (Reproduction Page 156)

Joe and Rhoda bought some items in the local pharmacy. All the items they bought cost the same amount, and they bought as many items as the number of cents in the cost of one single item. If Joe and Rhoda spent exactly $6.25, how many items did they buy?

Discussion

The first time students attempt this problem, they probably will focus on the fact that all of the items cost the same amount, and they spent $6.25. On the next reading, they should realize that Joe and Rhoda bought as many items as the cost of one item. That is, if the cost of the item was five cents, they bought five items. Finally, the students should realize that the problem concerns the square root of 6.25.

Problem 47 (Reproduction Page 157)

Guess my number!

(a) It is not a multiple of 2
(b) It is less than twice the square root of 1600
(c) It is the product of two prime numbers
(d) It is a multiple of 3
(e) It is greater than 8^2

Discussion

A list of possible answers should be developed with the class, from the clues:

Clues (b) and (e) place the number between 64 and 80.
Clue (a) eliminates all even numbers
Clue (d) retains only the multiples of 3

Thus the list would be 69 and 75, and only 69 is a product of two primes

$$69 = 23 \times 3$$

Problem 48 (Reproduction Page 157)

How many different squares can you find on a 6 × 6 checkerboard?

Discussion

Reduce the complexity and look for a pattern.

The first reaction to this problem is to say 36 squares. However, one quickly realizes that there are other squares, whose dimensions are 2 × 2, 3 × 3, etc. Begin with a 1 × 1 checkerboard and build up to a 6 × 6. Complete the table.

BOARD SIZE	NUMBER OF SQUARES						TOTAL
	1×1	2×2	3×3	4×4	5×5	6×6	
1×1	1	0	0	0	0	0	1
2×2	4	1	0	0	0	0	5
3×3	9	4	1	0	0	0	14
4×4	16						
5×5							
6×6	36	25	16	9	4	1	91

Problem 49 (Reproduction Page 158)

How many diagonals are there in a decagon?

Discussion

Draw and count, or reduce and look for a pattern.

Number of sides in polygon	Number of diagonals
3	0
4	2
5	5
6	9
7	14
8	20
9	27
10	35

Problem 50 (Reproduction Page 158)

A can with 40 nails in it weighs 135 grams, while the same can with only 20 nails in it weighs 75 grams. What is the weight of the can alone?

Discussion

Although this problem can easily be solved by considering the simultaneous solution of two equations, it can also be solved by logical reasoning. Since the can with 20 nails weighs 75 grams and the can with 40 nails weighs 135 grams, the extra 20 nails must supply the extra 60 grams. Thus each nail weighs 3 grams, and the can weighs 15 grams.

NAME: _____ DATE: _____

WHAT'S GOING ON?

On Thursday afternoon, Ann and Joe took their two children to the amusement park. They arrived at noon, and after riding on the ferris wheel and the roller coaster, they stopped for lunch. After lunch they took a boat ride through Mystery Canyon, and then went to the Petting Zoo. They left for home at 5:30 p.m.

1. Where did the family go?
2. What day of the week was it?
3. How many people went?
4. How many children went?
5. What time did they get there?
6. What rides did they go on before lunch?
7. What did they have for lunch?
8. Where did the boat ride take them?
9. Where did they go after the boat ride?
10. What time did they leave for home?

NAME: _____   DATE: _____

WHAT'S GOING ON?

Last February, Mr. and Mrs. Gonzalez took their three children on an airplane trip from their home in New York to visit their grandparents in Los Angeles. They took off from the airport in New York at 9:00 a.m., and arrived in Los Angeles airport at 11:30 a.m. (local time). While they were eating lunch, the pilot announced that they were over the Mississippi River. A little later on, the family was excited by a view of the Grand Canyon and the snow-capped Rockies.

1. In what city does the Gonzalez family live?

2. Where do the grandparents live?

3. What form of transportation did they use?

4. When did they leave New York?

5. When did they arrive in Los Angeles?

6. What river did they fly over during lunch?

7. What view excited them?

8. Which mountains were snow-capped?

9. Did they see the Grand Canyon before or after lunch?

NAME: _____ DATE: _____

WHAT'S GOING ON?

The basketball team at Shawnee Junior High School went to the big basketball game between the Los Angeles Lakers and the Philadelphia 76'ers. Dr. J.
of Philadelphia was the game's high scorer with 12 field goals (24 points) and
9 foul shots (9 points) for a total of 33 points. Magic Johnson was the high
scorer for Los Angeles with 31 points. The game was held up for 37 minutes
during the first half while they replaced a broken backboard.

1. Who went to the game?
2. Which teams played?
3. What kind of game was it?
4. Who was the high scorer in the game?
5. How many field goals did he score?
6. How many points did he score altogether?
7. Who was the high scorer for the Los Angeles Lakers?
8. How many points did he score?
9. When was the game help up?
10. For how long was the game held up?
11. Why was the game held up?
12. Who won the game?

NAME: _____   DATE: _____

RECOGNIZE THE WORD

Directions:

The first word on each line has been underlined. You are to put a circle around that same word *and only that exact word* every time it appears in that row.

Example:

(a) *sum*   some   (sum)   summation   (sum)

1.	add	addition	add	addend	add
2.	subtract	minus	submarine	substitute	subtract
3.	addition	add	additional	addend	admission
4.	answer	answer	anwar	answer	and so
5.	minus	minute	minimal	minus	mine
6.	multiply	multiple	multiply	multiplying	multiplier
7.	divide	division	divide	dividend	divisor
8.	remainder	remain	remnant	remainder	remand
9.	quotient	quote	quotient	quoting	quotient
10.	parentheses	parents	parentheses	parenthetical	parental

NAME: _____ **DATE:** _____

RECOGNIZE THE WORD

Directions:

The first word on each line has been underlined. You are to put a circle around that same word *and only that exact word* every time it appears in that row.

Example:

(a) <u>median</u>   medium   (median)   mediate   medial

1. <u>average</u>   average   averaged   averages   avenge
2. <u>median</u>   median   medium   median   medial
3. <u>mean</u>   meant   mean   measure   meen
4. <u>variation</u>   vary   variance   variety   varying
5. <u>sample</u>   simple   sampler   sampling   sample
6. <u>mode</u>   model   mode   moan   mode
7. <u>typical</u>   type   typist   typickal   typical
8. <u>statistics</u>   statistics   static   statistikal   statistician
9. <u>deviation</u>   device   defend   deviate   deviation
10. <u>scores</u>   snores   score   scores   scores

NAME: _____ **DATE:** _____

RECOGNIZE THE WORD

Directions:

Look through the forty-nine word array and try to match the words given below. When you find a match, put a circle around the word and record a tally mark in the proper place in the table. Find the total number of matches for each word. We have done the matches for "fraction" for you.

fraction   decimal   greater   smaller   product   ratio

(fraction)	decimal	grater	greater	decimal	product	smelt
descent	(fraction)	greater	smaller	smaller	faction	rate
product	product	(fraction)	decimal	ratio	return	greater
decimal	smaller	ratio	greatest	(fraction)	greater	protect
product	fracture	product	decent	smallest	smaller	rotate
decimal	small	great	(fraction)	ratio	decimal	ratio
smaller	fiction	ratio	smaller	produce	product	product

	fraction	decimal	greater	smaller	product	ratio
tally	ℍℍ					
number	5					

NAME: _____ DATE: _____

WHAT'S THE WORD?

Directions:

Select the one word from the list that belongs in both sentences of each pair. The word has a mathematical meaning in one sentence, and a non-mathematical meaning in the other.

CHORD	ROOT	EVEN	ODD	VOLUME	MEAN
POWER	DIFFERENCE	FACTOR		COUNT	PRIME

Example:

(a) That tree has a very _____ODD_____ shape.

(b) The numbers 1, 3, 7, and 17 are all _____ODD_____ numbers.

1. (a) Turn up the _____ on your stereo.

   (b) What is the _____ of that glass jar?

2. (a) A radish is the _____ of a plant.

   (b) Find the cube _____ of 27.

3. (a) _____ the number of apples in the box.

   (b) His Royal Highness the _____ of Transylvania.

4. (a) A _____ is a straight line that joins two points on a circle.

   (b) I'll play a 3-note _____ on the piano.

5. (a) The number 2 is the only even _____ .

   (b) The television program was scheduled in_____ time.

6. (a) The cruel stepmother was very _____ to the young girl.

   (b) The arithmetic _____ of the numbers 1, 5, 7, and 7 is 5.

7. (a) The _____ between 5 and 9 is 4.

   (b) There is no _____ whether you wear the blue one or the red one.

8. (a) The weather is a major _____ in your decision to go out or not.

   (b) 7 is a _____ of 28.

9. (a) Her quick rise to _____ made her the most powerful woman in all of Europe.

   (b) Raise x to the fourth _____ .

10. (a) The numbers 2, 4, 128, and 32 are all _____ numbers.

    (b) _____ the youngest child can play.

NAME: _____ DATE: _____

WHAT'S THE WORD?

Directions:

Find the words that complete each of the following pairs of sentences. A single word is to be used in each pair.

1. (a) The window was washed with a _____ of ammonia and water.

   (b) The _____ to the problem was to multiply the number of children by $1.50.

2. (a) Three is a member of the _____ of odd integers.

   (b) It took the pudding three hours to _____.

3. (a) "These are the _____ that try men's souls" is a well-known quotation.

   (b) Five _____ seven equals thirty-five.

4. (a) The seventy-seventh armored _____ was on maneuvers.

   (b) Johnny got the long _____ problem correct.

5. (a) Both of the doll's _____ were crushed by the car.

   (b) A right triangle has a hypotenuse and two _____.

6. (a) _____ the pump.

   (b) 17, 19, and 23 are all _____ numbers.

7. (a) The _____ of sets is all of the elements included in each set.

   (b) The members of the musician's _____ hold a picnic each year.

8. (a) The _____ of six and twelve is seventy-two.

   (b) The soap company gave away a coupon to encourage people to try their new _____.

NAME: _____ DATE: _____

WHAT'S THE QUESTION?

Directions:

For each of the following problems, check the question being asked.

Example:

Find the area of a rectangular room that is 50 feet in length and 25 feet wide.

What's the Question?

_____ What is the length of the room?
_____ What is the width of the room?
___X___ What is the area of the room?

1. Scott had $5.00. He bought three apples at 20¢ each and two ice cream cones at 70¢ each. How much money did Scott have left?

   What's the Question?

   _____ How much money did Scott spend on apples?
   _____ How much money did Scott spend on ice cream cones?
   _____ How much money did Scott have left after he made his purchases?
   _____ How much money did Scott spend?

2. A living room is in the form of a square that is 12 feet on each side. How much of the floor is left uncovered if there is a square carpet on the floor that is 9 feet by 9 feet?

   What's the Question?

   _____ How large is the room?
   _____ What is the area of the rug?
   _____ How many square feet are left uncovered?
   _____ How much does the rug cost?

3. A boy helped his father carry some cartons of paint into the shed. He carried three cartons each time he made a trip. If he carried a total of 34 cartons, how many trips did he make?

What's the Question?

_____ How many trips did the boy make?
_____ How many cartons did he carry?
_____ How many cartons did he carry on each trip?

4. Johnny has 6 apples, Jennifer has 11 apples, and Jules has 3 apples. They put all their apples together and sell them at 2 apples for 45¢. How much money do they take in if they sell all the apples?

What's the Question?

_____ How many apples did Jules have?
_____ How many apples did they have together?
_____ How much money will they have if they sell all the apples?

5. The temperature in the early morning was −5° Farenheit. During the day it rose 32° What temperature was reached?

What's the Question?

_____ What was the temperature early in the morning?
_____ What was the temperature later in the day?
_____ How much did the temperature rise during the day?

6. John can clean a swimming pool by himself in 6 hours. If he works together with Jeff, they can do the entire job in 4 hours. How long does it take Jeff to do the entire job alone?

What's the Question?

_____ How long does it take John to clean the swimming pool alone?
_____ How long does it take Jeff to clean the swimming pool alone?
_____ How long does it take them to clean the swimming pool together?
_____ How many gallons of water does it take to fill the swimming pool?

NAME: _____   DATE: _____

WHAT'S THE QUESTION?

Directions:

In each of the following problems, underline the question that is being asked.

1. A fisherman leaves the harbor at 4:00 a.m. and arrives at his nets in 3 hours. How long did it take him to travel from the harbor to his nets?

2. Find the amount of fencing needed to enclose a rectangular field whose dimensions are 250 meters by 45 meters.

3. By how many points did the Tigers defeat the Rams if the final score was Tigers 116, Rams 94?

4. George had $755.60 in his checking account. How much remained after he wrote checks in the amount of $18.18, $35.27, and $246 58?

5. After the tennis match, the four contestants went to an ice cream parlor. Two of them ordered chocolate sundaes while the other two ordered vanilla frappes. The bill of $4.56 was shared equally. How many people paid for ice cream?

6. Mike left for his summer home on Sunday morning at 9:30 a.m. His sister followed him, but she left at 11:45 a.m. on Sunday. How fast did his sister travel if they both arrived at the home at 6:15 p.m., and the home is 375 miles away?

NAME: _____ DATE: _____

WHAT'S THE QUESTION

Directions:

In each of the following, you are presented with a problem situation. Supply the question that makes each situation into a problem.

1. Marie and her father went to the baseball game last Sunday. They each ate two hot dogs and two soft drinks. The hot dogs cost 95¢ each, while the soft drinks cost 45¢ each. The admission to the ball park was $4.40 for adults and $2.20 for children. There were 45,000 fans at the game.

What's the Question? _____

_____

2. Keri and Kim spent all day Saturday shopping in the local shopping center. Keri bought a pair of blue jeans for $22.60 and a shirt for $11.95. Kim had $23.50 to spend, but he only bought a shirt for $14.95.

What's the Question? _____

_____

3. Sam and Dave drove to Georgia from their home, a distance of 832 miles. They bought 18 gallons of gasoline on the first day. They drove 388 miles the second day. They spent $22 for food on each day.

What's the Question? _____

_____

4. George Johnson can type a paper at the rate of 45 words per minute, while a word-processor can produce 250 words per minute. An assignment was made in class to write a 5,000 word term paper.

What's the Question? _____

_____

5. Lucille is planning to sell her collection of baseball cards which contains 1,250 cards. She has cards representing all the teams and all positions. She has 278 cards of pitchers, of which 113 are left handed. She has 31 catchers and 531 infielders.

What's the Question? _____

_____

6. The WHAT was giving a live performance at the fairgrounds. The concert began at 1:00 p.m. and lasted until 4:45 p.m. The group took two twenty-minute breaks. The concert consisted of 31 different selections.

What's the Question? _____

_____

NAME: _____ DATE: _____

WHAT ARE THE FACTS?

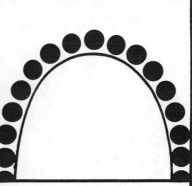

AT THE FAIRGROUNDS
HART BROTHERS CIRCUS
PERFORMANCE TODAY AT 1:30 P.M.

ADMISSION
ADULTS: $4.50
CHILDREN
UNDER 12 : $2.50
GATES OPEN AT 12:00

1. What event is taking place this afternoon?

2. Where is it taking place?

3. What time does it start?

4. What is the admission charge for a fourteen year old?

5. How much does an eleven year old pay?

6. Juanita got in line at 11:00 a.m. How long must she wait until the gates open?

7. Eric entered the fairgrounds at 12:15. How long does he wait until the performance begins?

8. The show ended at 4:45 p.m. How long was the performance?

9. Mrs. Schultz took her 4th grade class of 23 children to the circus. How much was the total admission?

NAME: _____   DATE: _____

WHAT ARE THE FACTS?

SANYO'S SPORTS SHOP

BIKE
HELMET
$38.50

BICYCLE
$225

TENNIS SHOES
$34.95

SHORTS
$5.95

TENNIS
RACKET
$45.98

SALE 15% OFF
ON EVERYTHING

1. How much is the regular price of the bicycle?

2. How much is the regular price of the tennis shoes?

3. Before the sale, what item sold for $45.98?

4. By how much were the prices reduced during the sale?

5. Mr. Clarke bought a bicycle and a bike helmet before the sale. How much did he spend?

6. Mrs. Lane bought a bicycle and a bike helmet during the sale. How much did she spend?

7. Peter bought a tennis racket and tennis shoes before the sale. How much did he spend?

8. Kenny bought a tennis racket and tennis shoes during the sale. How much did he spend?

NAME: _____ DATE: _____

WHAT ARE THE FACTS?

The guests at Marge's Sweet Sixteen party were having lunch. The meal prepared for the seventeen girls consisted of a fruit cup, tomato stuffed with chicken salad, cold asparagus, cole slaw, a beverage, and a parfait for dessert. After the lunch, Marge opened her gifts. Three of her friends had bought her a leather overnight case. She also received a lighted makeup mirror, four record albums, two sweaters, a gold bracelet from her parents, two pairs of earrings, a pair of gloves, and a transistor radio.

1. How many people had lunch at the party?
2. What did they have for dessert?
3. What material was the overnight case made from?
4. How many record albums did Marge receive?
5. What did her parents give her?
6. What kinds of jewelry did Marge receive?
7. How old was Marge?
8. How many guests were at the party?

NAME: _____ DATE: _____

WHAT ARE THE FACTS?

Gary and George, the Baker twins, left the house at 10:00 in the morning to go to the baseball game which started at 1:00 p.m. Their mother packed their lunch, consisting of two roast beef sandwiches, two egg salad sandwiches, two peanut butter and jelly sandwiches, and two apples. They arrived at the ballpark at 11:00, in time for batting practice. After the visiting team had their batting practice, Gary decided to eat a roast beef sandwich. Fifteen minutes later, George ate a peanut butter and jelly sandwich. At 12:30, both teams went to the locker room, and the groundskeepers began to prepare the field for the game. At that time, each boy ate an egg salad sandwich, Gary had a Coke, and George had a Seven-Up. During the game, they ate what was left of their lunch.

1. Where did the Baker twins spend their afternoon?
2. At what time did they leave their house?
3. When did Gary eat a roast beef sandwich?
4. When did George eat a peanut butter and jelly sandwich?
5. At what time did the teams go to the locker room?
6. When did they eat the egg salad sandwiches?
7. If Gary is fourteen years old, how old is George?
8. Who won the game?
9. How long did the groundskeepers have to get the field ready for the game?

NAME: _____   DATE: _____

MAKE UP THE PROBLEM

Jeff got all his word problems correct. His work is shown below. Can you think of word problems that match his work? Write your problem in the space provided next to each solution.

JEFF'S WORK		YOUR WORD PROBLEM
1. $\begin{array}{r} 258 \\ -194 \\ \hline 64 \end{array}$ My answer is 64 miles.		
2. $\begin{array}{r} 25 \\ \times 12 \\ \hline 50 \\ 250 \\ \hline 300 \end{array}$ My answer is 300 eggs.		
3. $\begin{array}{r} 81 \\ 93 \\ 78 \\ \hline 252 \end{array}$ $\begin{array}{r} 84 \\ 3\overline{)252} \end{array}$ My average is 84		

	JEFF'S WORK	YOUR WORD PROBLEM

4.

$$
\begin{array}{r}
8 \\
36\overline{)288} \\
288 \\
\hline
0
\end{array}
$$

My answer is 8 buses.

5.

$$
\begin{array}{r}
\$1.16 \\
.83 \\
1.79 \\
.72 \\
.18 \\
\hline
\$4.68
\end{array}
$$

$$
\begin{array}{r}
\$5.00 \\
-4.68 \\
\hline
.32
\end{array}
$$

She received 32¢ change.

NAME: _____   DATE: _____

MAKE UP THE PROBLEM

Directions:

Most of the time in school, the teacher or the textbook gives you the problem, and you have to supply the answer. Let's change things around. Here are the answers. For each of these answers, you make up a problem.

1. The answer is 103.   *Problem:* _____

    _____

    _____

2. The answer is 7 carrots.   *Problem:* _____

    _____

    _____

3. The answer is 45 miles   *Problem:* _____
   per hour.

    _____

    _____

4. The answer is the Los Angeles *Problem:* _____
   Dodgers.

    _____

    _____

5. The answer is David.   *Problem:* _____

    _____

    _____

6. The answer is 14 goldfish.   *Problem:* _____

_____

_____

7. The answer is $5.47.   *Problem:* _____

_____

_____

8. The answer is 1/2.   *Problem:* _____

_____

_____

9. The answer is 15 minutes.   *Problem:* _____

_____

_____

10. The answer is 7 pounds.   *Problem:* _____

_____

_____

NAME: _____   DATE: _____

MAKE UP THE PROBLEM

Directions:

Most of the time in school, the teacher or the textbook gives you the problem and you have to supply the answer. Let's change things around. Here are the answers. For each of these answers, you make up a problem.

1. The area is 48 square feet.   *Problem:* _____

_____

_____

2. The angle contains 16°.   *Problem:* _____

_____

_____

3. The answer is 42%.   *Problem:* _____

_____

_____

4. The perimeter is 150 meters.   *Problem:* _____

_____

_____

5. The weight was 1600 pounds.   *Problem:* _____

_____

_____

6. The time was 1 hour and 15 minutes.

Problem: _____

_____

_____

7. She used 14 gallons of paint.

Problem: _____

_____

_____

8. It took 36,000 gallons.

Problem: _____

_____

_____

9. The plane landed at 4:15 p.m.

Problem: _____

_____

_____

10. It was .025 inches thick.

Problem: _____

_____

_____

NAME: _____ DATE: _____

Problem: _____

_____

NAME: _____ DATE: _____

Problem: _____

_____

NAME: _____ DATE: _____

Problem: _____

_____

NAME: _____ DATE: _____

WHAT'S EXTRA?

Directions:

Sometimes a problem gives you more information than you need in order to solve it. You must be able to decide which facts are extra. Read each of the problems that follow. Select the fact or facts that are not needed.

1. John has a collection of 43 model cars. Mary has 23 cars in her collection. One day Janet came to visit John and brought along her model cars. She has 37 cars in her collection. How many cars do the girls own?

   What's Extra?

   _____ How many cars John has
   _____ How many cars Janet has
   _____ How many cars Mary has

2. Lucy filled her gas tank before she left on her car trip. She refilled it after traveling 264 miles. She put 12.3 gallons of unleaded gasoline into the tank, and it cost her $18. How many miles does she get on one gallon of gasoline?

   What's Extra?

   _____ The number of miles Lucy traveled
   _____ The number of gallons of gasoline she filled up with
   _____ The cost of the gasoline

3. Hot dogs cost 85¢ each, hamburgers cost $1.25 each, french fries cost 72¢ a portion, while soft drinks cost 65¢ each. How much did Alice spend on her lunch if she ate a hamburger, french fries, and a soft drink?

   What's Extra?

   _____ The cost of a hot dog
   _____ The cost of a hamburger
   _____ The cost of a soft drink
   _____ The cost of a portion of french fries

4. On the Monday night football game, Tiger Jones ran for 142 yards and caught passes good for 78 more yards. He scored 3 touchdowns. What was his total yardage?

   What's Extra?

   _____ How many yards he ran
   _____ How many touchdowns he scored
   _____ How many yards he gained by catching passes

5. The school cycling club organized a bike marathon. 37 cyclists started the trip. The course covered 18 miles from the starting line out to the lake where they had a picnic lunch. After lunch, they returned to the starting point by a different route, which was 12 miles long. Only 26 cyclists finished the marathon. How much longer is the trip out to the lake than the trip back?

   What's Extra?

   _____ The distance out to the lake
   _____ The distance back from the lake
   _____ The number of people who started the marathon
   _____ The number of people who finished the marathon

6. Ben and Nancy went trout fishing. They started at 11:00 and fished for two hours when they stopped for lunch. After lunch they fished for another 1½ hours. Nancy caught 5 fish in the morning and Ben caught 6. In the afternoon, Ben caught another 6 fish, while Nancy only caught 4. The limit per person for one day of fishing is 15 fish. How many more fish could Ben catch without exceeding the limit?

   What's Extra?

   _____ What time Ben and Nancy left
   _____ How long they fished before lunch
   _____ How many fish Ben caught before lunch
   _____ How many fish Ben caught after lunch
   _____ How many fish Nancy caught before lunch
   _____ How many fish Nancy caught after lunch
   _____ How many fish are the daily limit

NAME: _____   DATE: _____

WHAT'S EXTRA?

Directions:

Sometimes a problem gives you more information than you need in order to solve it. You must be able to decide which facts are extra. Read each of the problems that follow. Select the fact or facts that are not needed.

1. The Drama Club is having a car wash to raise money. They charge $2.50 for each car. They worked from 9:00 a.m. to 4:00 p.m., and took in $90. The goal for the day was to take in $100. How much short of their goal were they?

   What's Extra?

   _____ The time they started
   _____ The time they finished
   _____ How much they charge per car
   _____ How much they took in
   _____ How much was their goal

2. The Leather Shop advertised a sale of up to 50% off on selected items. Lou bought a brown jacket for $55 that originally sold for $90. He paid for the jacket with a $100 bill. How much did he save by buying the jacket on sale?

   What's Extra?

   _____ The savings were up to 50%
   _____ The color of the jacket was brown
   _____ The original price of the jacket
   _____ The actual price of the jacket that Lou paid
   _____ That he paid for it with a $100 bill

3. A vegetable garden is in the shape of a rectangle that is 50 feet by 80 feet. One half of the space is planted with corn, while the other half is equally divided between tomatoes and peppers. Corn requires 2 square feet per plant, tomatoes require 4 square feet per plant, while peppers require 3 square feet per plant. How many square feet of the garden were devoted to tomatoes?

What's Extra?

_____ The shape of the garden
_____ The dimensions of the garden
_____ The number of square feet each corn plant requires
_____ The number of square feet each tomato plant requires
_____ The number of square feet each pepper plant requires
_____ What part of the garden is devoted to tomatoes
_____ What part of the garden is devoted to peppers
_____ What part of the garden is devoted to corn

4. The Hot Shot Basketball Team won last night's game by 14 points. The high scorer, Bob Magic, had 7 field goals and made 3 out of 4 foul shots. Richie Kaye had 3 field goals and made 4 out of 6 foul shots. Joel Lewis had 2 field goals and made all 5 foul shots he took. Which of the three players had the best foul shooting percent in the game?

What's Extra?

_____ The Hot Shots won by 14 points
_____ The number of foul shots Bob made
_____ The number of foul shots Bob attempted
_____ The number of field goals Bob made
_____ The number of foul shots Richie made
_____ The number of foul shots Richie attempted
_____ The number of field goals Richie made
_____ The number of foul shots Joel attempted
_____ The number of foul shots Joel made
_____ The number of field goals Joel made

NAME: _____   DATE: _____

WHAT'S EXTRA?

Directions:

Sometimes a problem gives you more information than you need in order to solve it. You must be able to decide what facts are extra. Read each of the problems that follow. Put a circle around those facts that you do *not* need to solve the problem.

1. Mrs. Rand's Algebra 1 class took an algebra test during the 4th period last Monday. George and Jane each scored 100%. Four of her students had 95%, while three students failed. The class average was 79%. There were 28 students who took the test. What was the teacher's name?

2. Pizza can be purchased for 75¢ a slice or $4.60 for a whole pizza that contains eight slices. A large soft drink costs 75¢. Six members of the Seminole basketball team ordered 24 slices and six cokes. After they finished their food, Larry said, "We could have saved some money if we had only ordered three whole pizzas instead." How much would they have saved?

3. The mortar between bricks in a building is composed of one part lime, one part cement, five parts sand, and three parts water. How much lime is needed if we use 20 ounces of sand?

4. Jose began painting his fence at 9:00 a.m. After working for three hours he was joined by his brother Felipe. Together they finished the job in 3½ hours more. It took 4½ gallons of paint which costs $8.50 a gallon. How much did the paint cost?

5. Find the perimeter of the triangle shown at the right.

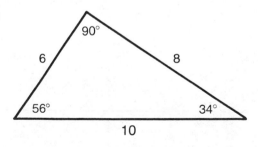

6. On Monday, Gregg delivered 47 copies of the *Inquirer*. He delivered twice as many copies on Sunday. The daily paper sells for 25¢, while the Sunday edition sells for 70¢. How much money did he collect for Sunday's papers?

7. The admission fee for the hockey exhibition game was $7.50 for adults and $4.00 for children under 14 years old. Mr. Stevens took his two daughters and their three friends to the game last Sunday. The admissions amounted to $27.50. How much change will he get from a $50 bill?

NAME: _____ DATE: _____

WHAT'S EXTRA?

Directions:

Sometimes a problem gives you more information than you need in order to solve it. You must be able to decide what facts are extra. Read each of the problems that follow. Put a circle around those facts that you do *not* need to solve the problem.

1. George was working at the corner grocery store on afternoons and weekends. His salary was $2.25 per hour and he averaged 18 hours of work each week. He saved most of his earnings, and has $83 in his savings account. He decided to buy a ten-speed bike that was on sale at the local sport shop for $189. How many weeks must he work in order to pay for the bike?

2. A TWA jet leaves New York for Los Angeles at 9:00 a.m. It is scheduled to arrive in Los Angeles at 11:30 a.m. The plane has a cruising speed of 550 miles an hour and is facing a head wind of 75 miles per hour. What is the scheduled flight time?

3. In a survey taken at the local bookstore last November, 2/5 of all the books sold were mysteries; 1/8 of those sold were westerns; 3/10 were science fiction; 1/20 were cookbooks, and the rest were miscellaneous categories. If there were 16 science fiction books sold, how many westerns were sold?

4. In 1978, Mr. Smith bought a new car for $6700. Four years later he sold it to a dealer for $1600. During the time he owned the car, Mr. Smith drove it 82,560 miles. How much did the car depreciate over the four year period?

5. Marty left her house in Baltimore at 8:00 a.m. to drive to New York City, a distance of 210 miles. She averages 50 miles per hour, and stops for one hour for lunch. If she uses 8.7 gallons of gasoline for the trip, how many miles per gallon did she average?

6. Craig is trying to beat the dealer in the card game of 21. He wants to get as close as he can to 21 without going over. He has a 7 and a 10, while Nancy has a 5 and an 8. Craig pulls a 2, and Nancy pulls a 6. The dealer stops with a 10 and a 9. How much does Craig need on his next card to win?

7. In the right triangle ABC, the m ∠ A = 30°. The length of side BC = 15 inches and the length of the hypotenuse is 30″. How large is ∠ B?

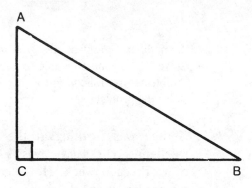

NAME: _____ DATE: _____

Directions:

Here is a table from the television guide for a Sunday evening of prime time viewing. Answer the following questions based on the information contained in the table.

	7:00	7:30	8:00	8:30	9:00	9:30	10:00	10:30
3	Disney's Wonderful World		CHiPs		Nero Wolfe		NBC Magazine	
6	Those Amazing Animals		Dr. Zhivago (Film)					
10	60 Minutes		Archie Bunker's Place	One Day at a Time	Alice	The Jeffersons	Trapper John, M.D.	
12	Together With Maria Callas		The Greatest Adventure		Boston Pops Special			
17	Star Trek		The Big Country (Film)					
29	M.A.S.H.	M.A.S.H.	Basketball—N.C.A.A. Final					
48	Love Story (Film)							News

1. Which channels had a movie during the evening?
2. Which channel had the greatest number of programs during the evening?
3. On which channel would you find "Archie Bunker's Place"?
4. What was showing on channel 48 at 9:00?
5. On what channel was the "Boston Pops Special"?
6. Which program was on twice during the evening?
7. Which movie was longer, *Dr. Zhivago* or *Love Story*?
8. How long is the program "The Greatest Adventure"?

NAME: _____   DATE: _____

RAMONA HIGH SCHOOL
MISS BATTISTA–9th GRADE
ATTENDANCE–WEEK OF APRIL 5th

M-5th		T-6th		W-7th		TH-8th		F-9th	
B	: G	B	: G	B	: G	B	: G	B	: G
13	14	12	12	16	11	14	13	16	14
27		24		27		27		30	

1. What situation does this table describe?

2. On what day was the class attendance best?

3. On what day was the class attendance worst?

4. On what day were there more girls in class than there were boys?

5. What was the average daily attendance for the week?

6. On Tuesday, what percent of those in attendance were girls?

7. Does the table tell you how many students there are in Miss Battista's class?

8. What is the lowest number of students that could be in Miss Battista's class?

NAME: _____ DATE: _____

BOX SCORE FOR THE MARLINS

Player's name and position	AB	R	H	2B	3B	HR	RBI	PO	A	E
Masters, 2B	5	3	3	1	0	0	0	1	6	0
Johnson, LF	5	1	1	0	0	0	0	4	0	0
Carey, RF	4	0	1	0	0	0	1	0	5	1
Cook, 3B	4	2	3	1	0	1	3	2	4	1
McDougald, 1B	3	0	0	0	0	0	1	10	1	0
Darryl, CF	4	0	0	0	0	0	0	4	0	0
Brooks, C	4	1	1	0	0	1	1	6	1	0
Brentwood, SS	4	0	1	0	0	0	1	0	8	0
Stevens, P	4	0	0	0	0	0	0	0	0	0
TOTALS	37	7	10	2	0	2	7	27	25	2

1. Who was the shortstop for the Marlins? Who was their second baseman?

2. Which player had the fewest official at-bats?

3. Which player or players hit a home run?

4. How many doubles were hit?

5. How many hits did the Marlins get in this game?

6. How many runs did Cook score?

7. Who scored the most runs?

8. What was the team batting average for this game?

NAME: _____   DATE: _____

MILEAGE BETWEEN MAJOR CITIES

Directions:

Here is a table of distances between certain cities within the United States. Answer the following questions based on the information contained in the table.

	Atlanta	Chicago	Dallas	El Paso	Little Rock	Los Angeles	New Orleans	Philadelphia
Atlanta	X	715	839	1476	362	2289	523	797
Chicago	715	X	971	1483	660	2128	957	757
Dallas	839	971	X	630	343	1450	504	1544
El Paso	1476	1483	630	X	880	810	1124	2132
Little Rock	362	2128	343	880	X	1710	438	1200
Los Angeles	2289	2128	1450	810	1710	X	1937	2874
New Orleans	523	957	504	1124	438	1937	X	1276
Philadelphia	797	757	1544	2132	1200	2874	1276	X

1. How many miles is it from Los Angeles to El Paso?

2. How many miles is it from Los Angeles to Philadelphia?

3. Which is further from Little Rock, Dallas or New Orleans?

4. Which of the cities in the table is closest to Philadelphia?

5. How much further is it from Dallas to Atlanta, than from Los Angeles to El Paso?

6. The Kent family is traveling from their home in New Orleans to visit friends in Los Angeles. They want to make one stopover. Which trip is shorter, traveling by way of Dallas, or by way of Little Rock?

NAME: _____ DATE: _____

CALORIE AND CARBOHYDRATE TABLES

Food and amount	Calories	Carbohydrates
Apple (average size, raw, unpeeled)	66	17
Banana (average size)	87	23
Bread (white, one slice)	62	12
Peanut butter (one tablespoon)	82	3
Popcorn (one cup without butter)	43	9
Cola Drink (8-ounce cup)	96	25
Milk (8 ounce cup)	159	12
Jelly (grape, 1 teaspoon)	16	4
Chicken (4 ounces, broiled)	155	0
Beef (4 ounces, broiled)	326	0

Here is a table that shows the number of calories and the number of grams of carbohydrates in a portion.

1. For each of the following snacks, determine the number of calories and grams of carbohydrates.

    (a) beef hamburger (4 ounces, no bread)
    cup of milk (8 ounces)
    apple (one, average)

    (b) broiled chicken (4 ounces)
    cola drink (8 ounces)
    white bread (2 slices)
    banana (1)

    (c) peanut butter and jelly sandwich
    3 tablespoons of peanut butter
    2 teaspons of grape jelly
    2 slices of white bread
    milk (8 ounce cup)

    (d) popcorn (one cup, no butter)
    peanut butter (2 tablespoons)
    white bread (2 slices)
    banana (1, average)

2. Prepare a "snack menu" that includes no more than 85 grams of carbohydrates. You may include as many foods as you like. Then find the total number of calories your snack contains.

NAME: _____ DATE: _____

"J" TEAM BASKETBALL BOX SCORE

PLAYER'S NAME	FGA	FG	FA	F	TP	PF
Jeanne	7	4	4	3		2
Josephine	12	9	7		24	4
Joan	2		0	0	2	1
Jerri		4	2	0	8	
Julie		4			11	1
Jane	9					
TOTALS	48	29	23	17	75	15

FGA = Field Goals Attempted
FG = Field Goals Made (2 points)
FA = Foul Shots Attempted

F = Foul Shots Made (1 point)
TP = Total Points
PF = Personal Fouls

1. Use the information below to complete the table
   (a) Jerri attempted 10 field goals and committed 3 personal fouls.
   (b) Jane made five field goals and all her foul shot attempts.
   (c) Julie made half of her field goal attempts and 3 out of the 5 foul shots she was awarded.

2. Answer each of the following. (A calculator would be useful.)
   (a) What was the team's average in shooting field goals? (State your answer as a percent.)
   (b) What was Jane's average for shooting foul shots? (State your answer answer as a percent.)
   (c) What player had the best field goal average?

NAME: _____   DATE: _____

SAM'S SPORTING GOODS

ITEM	NUMBER ON HAND	UNIT COST	VALUE
Baseballs			
Bats			
Catcher's Gloves			
First Baseman's Gloves			
Fielder's Gloves			

Sam's Sporting Goods Store has on hand 182 baseballs, 16 first baseman's gloves, 86 bats, 74 fielder's gloves, and 12 catcher's gloves. The bats cost Sam $9.25 each, the catcher's gloves cost $32.50 each, fielder's gloves cost $24.87 each, baseballs cost $2.87 each, and the first baseman's gloves cost $19.95 each.

1. Complete the table showing Sam's inventory.

2. What is the value of the baseballs in Sam's shop?

3. Which are worth more, Sam's inventory of catcher's gloves or his inventory of first basemen's gloves?

4. What is the total value of Sam's inventory?

NAME: _____   DATE: _____

THE ALGEBRA TEST

Here are the scores made by the 9th grade algebra class on their test, along with a frequency table:

87, 64, 92, 71, 95, 85, 85, 86, 99, 65, 73, 58, 63, 89,
92, 87, 85, 68, 84, 85, 69, 73, 71, 74, 92, 90, 73, 95

Complete the table (we have entered the first five tallies for you) and answer the following questions.

RANGE OF SCORES	TALLY	FREQUENCY
95–99	I	
90–94	I	
85–89	I	
80–84		
75–79		
70–74	I	
65–69		
60–64	I	
55–59		

1. How many points are in each interval?
2. How many students took the test?
3. Which interval has the most scores?
4. Which interval has the fewest scores?
5. Which intervals have the same number of scores?
6. Find the class average. (Your calculator will help.)

NAME: _____   DATE: _____

THE STAMP DISPLAY

Mr. Carter, Mr. Rosen, Mr. Miller, Mrs. Bruce and Miss Newton are all members of the Temple Stamp Collector's Club. At a recent show, they displayed parts of their collections. The stamps they showed were postage dues, air mails, commemoratives, special deliveries, and revenues. Mr. Carter's display contained 25 airmails, 6 special deliveries, and 38 commemoratives. Mr. Rosen displayed 16 air mails, 15 special deliveries, 12 postage dues, and 9 revenues. Mr. Miller showed 11 postage dues, 75 air mails, 16 revenues, and 45 special deliveries. Mrs. Bruce displayed 46 commemoratives and 112 air mails, while Miss Newton displayed 6 revenues, 17 commemoratives, 11 special deliveries, 43 air mails, and 21 postage dues.

Organize the data in table form and answer the following questions.

1. What was the total number of stamps that the five collectors displayed?

2. Which category had the highest representation?

3. Which category had the fewest stamps?

4. How many stamps did Mrs. Bruce display?

5. Who showed no commemoratives?

6. Which collector showed the most stamps?

7. Which collector showed the fewest stamps?

NAME: _____   DATE: _____

HOURS WORKED AT THE HAMBURGER SHOP

Last week, Ronnie, Barbara, Mabel and Paul all worked part time at the local hamburger shop. Ronnie worked 1½ hours on Monday, 2 hours on Tuesday, 3½ hours on Wednesday, and 7 hours on Saturday. Barbara worked 8 hours on Saturday and 8 hours on Sunday. Mabel worked 4 hours every day except Sunday, which was her day off. Paul worked 4 hours on Monday, 3 hours on Wednesday, 3 hours on Friday, and 6 hours on Saturday.

Organize the data in table form and answer the following questions.

1. Who worked the most hours last week?

2. Who worked the fewest hours last week?

3. Who worked on Saturday?

4. Who worked on Thursday?

5. At $3.25 an hour, how much did Barbara earn last week?

6. Ronnie earns $3.50 an hour, while Paul earns $3.35 an hour. Who earned more money last week? How much more?

NAME: _____ **DATE:** _____

COST OF LUNCH MEAT

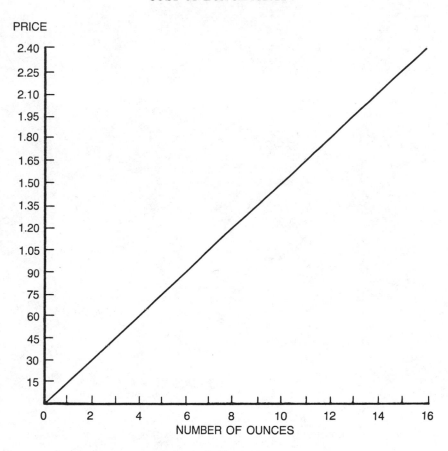

PRICE

This graph shows the cost of up to 16 ounces of luncheon meat.

1. How much would you pay for 3 ounces?
2. Jill spent $2.10 for luncheon meat. How many ounces did she buy?
3. How much would you pay for one-half pound?
4. How much would you pay for 3/4 of a pound?
5. At this same rate, how much would you pay for 1½ pounds?

NAME: _____ DATE: _____

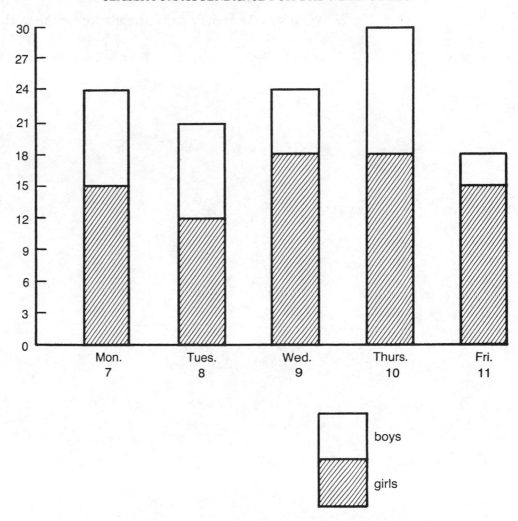

CLASSROOM ATTENDANCE FOR THE WEEK OF MAY 7

This graph shows the classroom attendance of a 9th grade class for the week of May 7–11. There are 18 girls and 12 boys in the class.

1. On which day was everyone in class?

2. On which day was the attendance poorest?

3. How many girls were present on Friday?

4. On what days were the same number of students present in class?

5. On what days were the same number of boys present?

6. On what day was the ratio of boys to girls present 1:3?

7. What was the average daily attendance for the week?

NAME: _____   DATE: _____

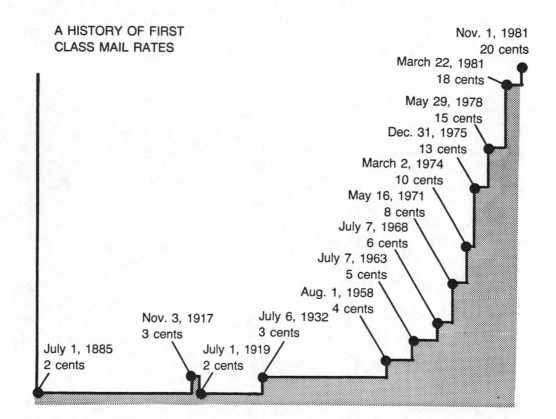

A HISTORY OF FIRST
CLASS MAIL RATES

Nov. 1, 1981
20 cents

March 22, 1981
18 cents

May 29, 1978
15 cents

Dec. 31, 1975
13 cents

March 2, 1974
10 cents

May 16, 1971
8 cents

July 7, 1968
6 cents

July 7, 1963
5 cents

Aug. 1, 1958
4 cents

Nov. 3, 1917
3 cents

July 6, 1932
3 cents

July 1, 1885
2 cents

July 1, 1919
2 cents

Here is a graph that shows the changes in first class postage rates since 1885. Each of the following questions involves mailing a one-ounce or less, first class letter.

1. How much did it cost to mail a letter on June 7, 1978?

2. How much did it cost to mail a letter on May 1, 1971?

3. Did it cost more to mail a letter on July 8, 1964, or July 8, 1969?

4. There were two different time periods when it cost only 2¢ to mail a letter. When were these two time periods?

5. On what date did the postage rate go to 10¢?

6. How much would you have saved if you mailed 23 invitations to your party on May 28, 1978, instead of on May 30, 1978?

NAME: _____   DATE: _____

EXPENSES OF A JUMBO BURGER SHOPPE

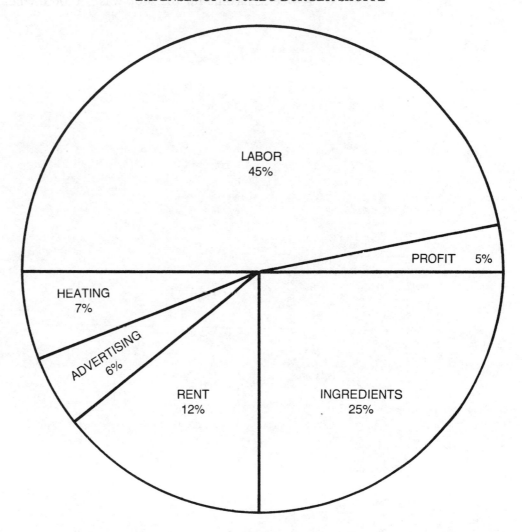

The circle graph shows the expenses of a burger shop.

1. What is the sum of the percent units shown on the graph?

2. What is the rate of profit?

3. What part of the expenses is used for the ingredients?

4. What part of the expenses goes towards rent?

5. On a two dollar order, how much is given over to labor?

6. A week's income for the shop was $20,000. What was their profit?

NAME: _____   DATE: _____

MAILING RATES FOR FIRST CLASS LETTERS

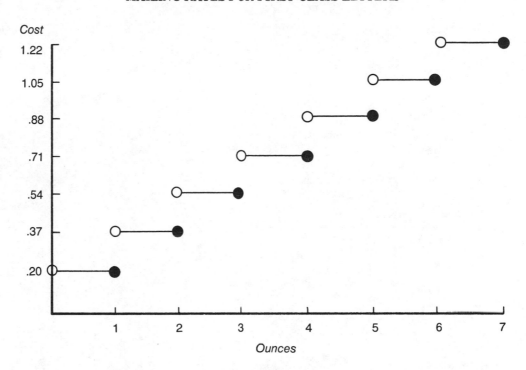

This graph shows the cost of mailing a first class letter in the United States as of December 1981. The rates are determined by the weight of the letter. Any letter weighing one ounce or less costs 20¢. Any letter greater than one ounce but less than or equal to two ounces costs 37¢ to mail.

1. Find the cost of mailing a letter that weighs 5 ounces.

2. Find the cost of mailing a letter that weighs 2½ ounces.

3. Find the cost of mailing a letter that weighs 2¾ ounces.

4. Find the cost of mailing a letter that weighs 4¾ ounces.

5. How much does a letter weigh if it costs $1.05 to mail?

6. How much does a letter weigh if it costs 71¢ to mail?

NAME: _____ DATE: _____

The Philadelphia 76'ers scored 120 points against the Indiana Pacers. The scoring was as follows:

Cureton	6 points
Malone	18 points
Erving	36 points
Cheeks	3 points
B. Jones	24 points
C. Johnson	12 points
Iavarone	3 points
Toney	18 points

Prepare a circle graph to show this distribution and give the percent of the total scored by each player.

NAME: _____   DATE: _____

Barbara was taking her annual stress test for the company exercise program. The doctor monitored her pulse rate every minute. She started at 72 beats per minute (bpm). After one minute of exercise it had reached 108 bpm. After two minutes of exercise it was 126 bpm. At the three minute point, when they stopped the treadmill, it had reached 156 bpm. After four minutes it dropped back to 144 bpm; after five minutes it was 120 bpm. At the end of six minutes her pulse rate was 108 bpm. At the seven minute mark it was down to 96 bpm, and it was back to 72 bpm at the 10 minute mark.

Prepare a line graph to illustrate this information, and approximate Barbara's pulse rate after eight minutes.

NAME: _____ DATE: _____

Here is a chart showing the average monthly rainfall in Portland, Oregon and Springfield, Illinois.

	Jan	Feb	Mar	Apr	May	Jun	Jul	Aug	Sep	Oct	Nov	Dec
Portland	15	11	10	6	4	5	2	3	5	10	15	18
Springfield	5	4	7	10	8	10	7	8	8	6½	6	5

Construct a bar graph showing the data, and use the graph to answer the following questions.

1. How many centimeters of rain fell during the year in each city?
2. In which month was there the greatest difference in rainfall?
3. In which month was there the least difference in rainfall?
4. In what month was the rainfall in Portland three times the rainfall in Springfield?

NAME: _____ DATE: _____

Steve is responsible for keeping the fish tank in the "Seaside Aquarium Shop" filled. One of the fifty-gallon tanks has a slight leak. Along with evaporation, it loses two gallons of water each day. Every three days, Steve adds five gallons of water to the tank; after 30 days, he fills it. Prepare a graph to illustrate this data. How much water will Steve have to add on the 30th day to fill the tank?

NAME: _____ DATE: _____

DRAWING DIAGRAMS

Directions:

Use a drawing or diagram to represent the information included in each of the following problems. Then solve the problem.

1. A watermelon and two cantaloupes cost $4.65. Two watermelons and two cantaloupes cost $7.40. How much does one watermelon cost?

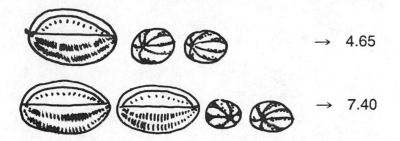

2. A photographer wishes to make a developer solution by mixing 3 parts of water with one part of chemical. How many ounces of chemical will the photographer use if he wishes to make 32 ounces of solution?

$$\boxed{W}\ \boxed{W}\ \boxed{W}\ \boxed{C} \rightarrow \ 4$$

3. For every two hamburgers that you buy, you get one free bottle of soda. How many bottles of soda do I get if I buy eight hamburgers?

4. An airplane has two empty seats for every three seats that are occupied. At this same rate, how many seats are occupied on an airplane that has room for 55 people?

5. At the entrance to the zoo there is a map. The various habitats are all

located along one path. The snakes are between the giraffes and the alligators. The alligators are between the elephants and the snakes. The first habitat that they came to was the giraffes'. What was the next habitat that they came to?

6. Vicksburg is south of Cooperstown but north of Leesburg. Trashville is due south of Vicksburg but due north of Leesburg. Yorkville is due north of Vicksburg but due south of Cooperstown. Which of the towns is second most northerly of the four?

NAME: _____ DATE: _____

DRAWING DIAGRAMS

Directions:

Use a drawing or a diagram to represent the information included in each of the following problems. Then solve the problem.

1. Bubbletown, Carterstown, Dinnersville and Huntsville all lie along a single straight road. Huntsville is west of Carterstown. Bubbletown is west of Dinnersville but east of Carterstown. Which town is the farthest east?

2. John is giving a picnic. For every 3 hot dogs, he will order 4 cokes. How many cokes should he order to go along with 12 hot dogs?

3. I place ten pennies in a row. Now I replace every third coin with a nickel. Then I replace every fourth coin with a dime. Finally, I replace every fifth coin with a quarter. What is the value of the ten coins that are now on the table?

4. Nancy is standing in her own backyard facing north. She turns 90° to her right, then 180° additional to her right. Then she turns 90° to the left, and then turns through 360°. In which direction is she now facing?

5. Four families are driving on the same road to Las Vegas. The Millers saw the Randolphs in front of them. The Jones passed the Koopers just before entering town. The Randolphs are between the Millers and the Koopers. Who arrived first?

DRAWING DIAGRAMS

Directions:

Use a drawing or a diagram to represent the information included in each of the following problems. Then solve the problem.

1. A basketball team with 14 players has the players listed at three positions: center, forward and guard. When the manager counts the centers and guards, she counts eight players. When she counts the forwards and the centers, she counts nine players. How many centers, how many forwards, and how many guards are on the team?

2. In a plane, line a is parallel to line b; line b is perpendicular to line c; line c is parallel to line d, while line e is perpendicular to line d. What relationship does line e have to line a?

3. There are 18 students standing in a circle, evenly spaced and consecutively numbered. Which student is directly opposite student number 1?

4. The students in a seance are seated around a circular table, evenly spaced and consecutively numbered. Student number 5 is directly opposite student number 16. How many students are at the table?

5. Two trains leave Junction City at 10:00 a.m. The Flyer travels due north at 60 miles per hour, while the Comet travels due west. After two hours they were 150 miles apart. How fast was the Comet traveling?

NAME: _____   DATE: _____

DRAWING DIAGRAMS

Directions:

Use a drawing or a diagram to represent the information included in each of the following problems. Then solve the problem.

1. Six students are sitting at a table that is in the shape of a regular hexagon. If Charles is next to Francine, Alice is across from Charles, and Benjy is between Alice and Emily, who is across from Dennis?

2. At a circular table, Jeff is between Mike and Peter. Alex is between Louis and David. Louis is between Alex and Mike, and Peter is between Jeff and David. Who sits on either side of Mike?

3. How many diagonals are there in a hexagon?

4. Stan starts at point A and walks 30 meters due south to point B. He then turns through 90° and walks 40 meters due east to point C. He pauses, and then continues on in the same direction for 20 more meters to point D. He turns south again and walks due south for 50 meters, to point E. How far is point E directly from point A?

5. There are 10 dials in a row, all pointing to 12:00. The first student walks past each dial and turns them all through 90 degrees to point to 3:00. The second student then walks by and turns every even-numbered dial through 90 degrees to point to 6:00. The third student then walks through and turns every third dial (numbers 3, 6, and 9) through 90 degrees additional. The fourth student turns every fourth dial (numbers 4 and 8) through an additional 90 degrees. The fifth student turns every fifth dial (numbers 5 and 10) through an additional 90 degrees, and so on until all ten students have walked by and turned the dials. After all ten students have "done their thing" which dials are now pointing to 12:00?

NAME: _____ DATE: _____

SYMBOLS AND WORDS

Directions:

You and your partner are to discuss each of the statements on this sheet. You must decide whether you agree (A) or disagree (D) with the statement, and place an (A) or a (D) next to that statement.

Example:

_____ $\sqrt{10}$ _____	is read as "the square root of ten."	A
1. _____ $7 + 12$ _____	is read as "the product of seven and twelve."	_____
2. _____ $7 - 18$ _____	is read as "seven subtracted from eighteen."	_____
3. _____ $32 + 9$ _____	is read as "the sum of thirty-two and nine."	_____
4. _____ $7 \div 5 = 1, R\ 2$ _____	is read as "the remainder when seven is divided by five is two."	_____
5. _____ $8 - 5$ _____	is read as "the difference between eight and five."	_____
6. _____ 8×5 _____	is read as "the product of eight and five."	_____
7. _____ $9 < 6$ _____	is read as "nine is greater than six."	_____
8. _____ $12 \neq 24/2$ _____	is read as "twelve does not equal twenty-four halves."	_____
9. _____ $7 \geqslant 9$ _____	is read as "seven is greater than or equal to nine."	_____
10. _____ $8 = 6 + 2$ _____	is read as "eight increased by six equals two."	_____

NAME: _____   DATE: _____

SYMBOLS AND WORDS

Directions:

You and your partner are to discuss each of the statements on this sheet. Then fill in the blank with the correct symbolic or verbal statement.

Example:

5×7 is read as "the product of five and seven" or "five times seven."

1. _____ is read as "the sum of five and twelve."

2. 6×3 is read as " _____ ."

3. $4 - 2$ is read as " _____ ."

4. _____ is read as "seventeen multiplied by three."

5. _____ is read as "the square root of twenty-five."

6. $19 > 17$ is read as " _____ ."

7. _____ is read as "twelve is less than or equal to seven plus six."

8. _____ is read as "the product of nine and three, increased by four."

9. $137 \div 13$ is read as " _____ ."

10. _____ is read as "the fourth power of x."

NAME: _____ DATE: _____

ALGEBRAIC EXPRESSIONS

I. Directions:

In each of the following, select an appropriate variable or variables. Represent each statement algebraically. In some cases, a diagram can be used. Do not solve.

1. John is five years older than Mary.

2. Paul has twice as much money as Sally.

3. Smithville and Absecon are thirteen miles apart.

4. Three-fourths of the class were girls.

5. Five people shared a box of cookies equally. How many does each one get?

6. The cost of seven cans of soup is $1.82.

7. The number of hours it takes to drive 150 miles at 35 miles per hour.

8. The number of people who came to Jerry's party if four families each had three members and three families each had four members.

9. Bernie and Ann bought 23 cupcakes. Bernie bought five more than Ann.

10. The sum of the measures of the angles of triangle ABC is 180°.

II. Directions:

Write a sentence or sentences for which each of the following would be the algebraic representation.

1. $x + y = 12$

2. $2x = 17$

3. $6T + 6 + 3F$

4. $n - 18$

5. $460 \div n = 5$

NAME: _____   DATE: _____

ALGEBRAIC EXPRESSIONS

Directions:

For each of the following write a mathematical expression.

1. Twenty-seven more than the number n.

2. The amount that each of four people pay for a pizza that costs x.

3. George's age if he is five years older than Marlene who is y years old.

4. The cost of seven tropical fish if each fish costs m dollars.

5. The number of books on n shelves if there are 30 books on each shelf.

6. The distance traveled in four hours at a speed of r miles per hour.

7. The number of heartbeats in m minutes for a person whose heart beats at 72 beats per minute.

8. The weight of one package of bubble gum if p packages weigh 18 ounces.

9. The number of points scored by a football team which scored three touchdowns, three extra points, and f field goals.

10. The third side of a triangle whose perimeter is p and two of whose sides are 3 and 4.

11. The number of rock records Juanita has in her collection, if she has x records and 30% of them are rock.

12. The area of a rectangle whose width is 3 and whose length is 9.

13. The number of jars needed to can g tomatoes if each jar contains 6 tomatoes.

14. The number of tennis balls manufactured in h hours if they are manufactured at the rate of 12,000 per hour.

15. The number of people on two ferryboats if one has 362 people and the other has x people.

NAME: _____   DATE: _____

THE TRACK MEET

Directions:

Read the following paragraphs very carefully. The answers to the questions listed below are contained in the paragraphs. Do your best to answer each question.

Mr. and Mrs. Newton and their n children went to the fairgrounds to see the local track meet. They left their house at 8:00 a.m. and arrived at t. They put their car in the parking lot which charged $1.25 an hour. The cost of admission was $3 for adults and $2 for children.

The first event was a 100-yard dash. The winner ran the race in m seconds, one second ahead of the runner-up. The next event was the broad jump. The winner jumped one inch less than the world record, w.

The family decided to beat the crowd and have an early lunch. Mr. Newton bought eight hamburgers at B cents each, two large french fries at 80¢ each and d soft drinks at 55¢ each.

After lunch, they went to watch the four-man relay race. The runners on the winning team ran their laps in 59 seconds, 50 seconds, 58 seconds, and s seconds. It began to rain, so the Newtons decided to leave early. They drove out of the parking lot at 4:00 p.m.

1. Represent the number of people, F, in the Newton family.

2. Represent the length of the trip, L, to the fairgrounds.

3. Represent the cost, C, for the family to enter the track meet.

4. Represent the time, H, it took the second-place runner to run the 100-yard dash.

5. Represent the length, J, of the winning broad jump.

6. Represent the cost, A, of the hamburgers the Newton family had for lunch.

7. Represent the number of hamburgers each child ate, if each parent had one hamburger and the children shared the rest of them equally.

8. Represent the cost of the lunch, E.

9. Represent the number of seconds, S, it took the fourth runner to run the final lap of the relay race.

10. Represent the winning time, X, for the relay race.

11. Represent the average time, I, for each member of the winning relay team.

12. Represent the cost, P, of parking the car for the day.

NAME: _____ DATE: _____

PATTERNS

Directions:

For each of the following, tell in your own words what the Pattern Rule is, and write another element.

1. apples, bananas, oranges, pears, _____

   Pattern Rule: _____

2. blue, red, purple, orange, _____

   Pattern Rule: _____

3. James, Joan, Jane, Jerry, _____

   Pattern Rule: _____

4. shoes, socks, coats, ties, _____

   Pattern Rule: _____

5. dogs, cats, cows, horses, _____

   Pattern Rule: _____

6. 2, 10, 28, 4, 16, _____

   Pattern Rule: _____

7. nickels, quarters, dimes, pennies, _____

   Pattern Rule: _____

8. Mississippi, Ohio, Amazon, Nile, _____

   Pattern Rule: _____

9. baseball, football, tennis, hockey, _____

   Pattern Rule: _____

10. a, e, i, o, _____

    Pattern Rule: _____

11. 1/2, 5/7, 3/8, 2/17, _____

    Pattern Rule: _____

12. 1-1/2, 2-3/4, 7-1/8, 3-5/9, _____

    Pattern Rule: _____

NAME: _____ **DATE:** _____

PATTERNS

Directions:

For each of the following, tell in your own words what the Pattern Rule is, and write the next term.

1. 2, 4, 6, 8, _____

   Pattern Rule: _____

2. a, ab, abc, _____

   Pattern Rule: _____

3. 1z, 2y, 3x, 4w, _____

   Pattern Rule: _____

4. a, do, boy, girl _____

   Pattern Rule: _____

5. 1, 2, 4, 7, 11, _____

   Pattern Rule: _____

6. 2, 3, 5, 8, 13, _____

   Pattern Rule: _____

7. Arlene, Bob, Charlotte, David, _____

   Pattern Rule: _____

8. 80, 40, 20, 10, _____

    Pattern Rule: _____

9. 2, 1, 4, 3, 6, 5, _____

    Pattern Rule: _____

10. , , , _____

    Pattern Rule: _____

11. J, F, M, A, _____

    Pattern Rule: _____

12. 1, 1, 2, 3, 5, _____

    Pattern Rule: _____

NAME: _____ DATE: _____

WHICH IS DIFFERENT?

Directions:

In each of the following sets, one element doesn't belong. Find which one is different and tell why it doesn't belong.

1. Washington, Jefferson, Lincoln, Franklin, Grant _____

2. 36, 75, 9, 81, 25 _____

3. △ , ○ , □ , ▭ , ⬡ _____

4. mom, noon, dog, dad, level _____

5. Styx, Beatles, Dodgers, Kansas, Stones _____

6. roll, beef, carrot, fish, lettuce _____

7. blue, black, orange, brown, beige _____

8. 6, 25, 18, 27, 33 _____

9. 3, 6, 9, 11, 15 _____

10. New Years, Halloween, July 4th, Thanksgiving, Christmas _____

NAME: _____ **DATE:** _____

WHAT'S NEXT?

Directions:

In each of the following, find the pattern and draw the next two figures.

1. ▽ □ ⬠ __ __

2. △ ◁▷ ◸◹ __ __

3. __ L △ □ __ __

4. ↓ ●→ ↥ __ __

5. □ , △ , □ □ , △ △ , □ □ □ __ , __

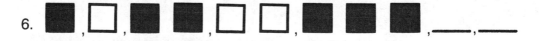

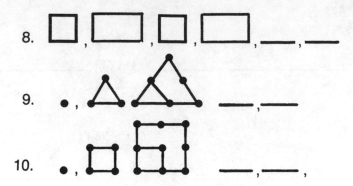

8. □ , ▭ , □ , ▭ , __ , __

9. • , △ , △ , __ , __

10. • , □ , ⊟ , __ , __ ,

NAME: _____ DATE: _____

ANALOGIES

Directions:

Look at each of the following. Notice how figure A changes to figure B. Now let figure C change in the same way. Put a circle around the result. The first one has been done for you.

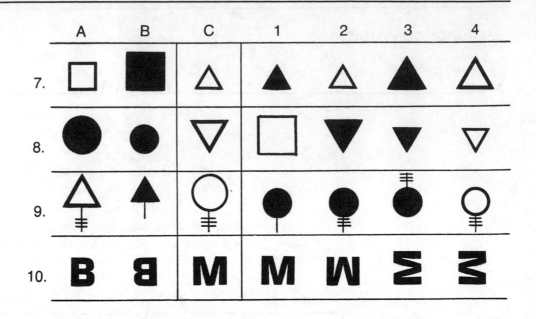

NAME: _____ DATE: _____

ANALOGIES

Directions:

Look at each of the following. Notice how figure A changes to figure B. Now let figure C change in the same way. Put a circle around the result.

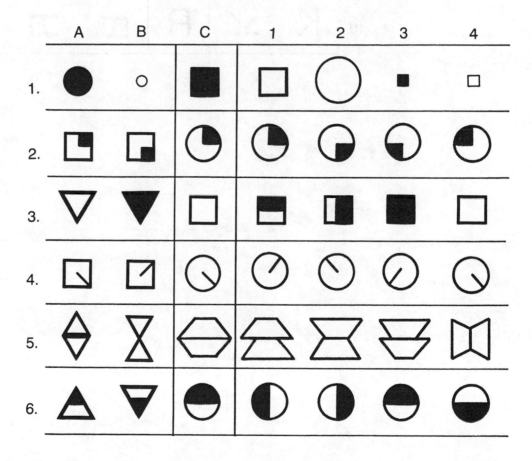

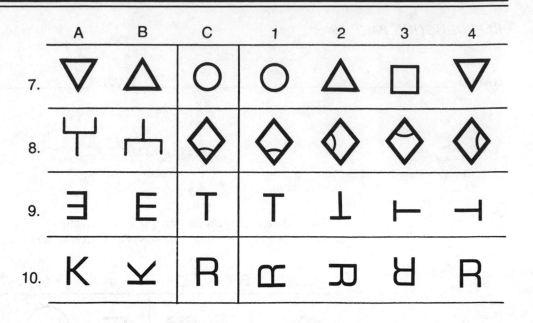

	A	B	C	1	2	3	4
7.	▽	△	○	○	△	□	▽
8.	Ψ	⊥	◇	◇	◇	◇	◇
9.	Ǝ	Ǝ	T	T	⊥	⊢	⊣
10.	K	⋏	R	Я	⅃	ᴚ	R

NAME: _____   DATE: _____

GRANDMOTHER'S LIKES AND DISLIKES

Here are some things that my grandmother likes and some things that she dislikes.

My grandmother likes apples, but dislikes oranges. She likes beef, but dislikes lamb. She likes teenagers, but dislikes children. She likes parrots, but dislikes cats and dogs. She likes cookies, but dislikes cakes and pies.

Which of the following would you say my grandmother likes?

OBJECT	LIKES	DISLIKES
pears		
veal		
copper		
brass		
bitter fruits		
sweet chocolate		
hot chocolate		
cool weather		
oceans		
swimming pool		

NAME: _____ DATE: _____

GRANDFATHER'S LIKES AND DISLIKES

Here are some things that my grandfather likes and some things that he dislikes.

My grandfather likes beef, but dislikes veal. He likes an abacus, but dislikes a calculator. He likes towels marked "HIS" and towels marked "HERS". He likes to sigh, but never to cry. He likes calm people, but he dislikes angry people. He likes Houston, but dislikes Dallas.

Which of the following would you say my grandfather likes?

OBJECT	LIKES	DISLIKES
stamps		
ferryboats		
tugboats		
Chinese food		
Mexican food		
notepaper		
gold		
flashlight		
rust		
roses		

NAME: _____ DATE: _____

THE PEN PAL CLUB

Dolores and Pat started a pen pal club. It was decided that once a month each member would send a letter to every member of the club. It was also decided to add one new member to the club each month. How many letters were mailed during the month in which the sixth member joined the club?

NAME: _____ DATE: _____

RECORD SALES

The REC Record Company just released a new album. The first week, they only received two orders. Then the album began to catch on. The second week they received 27 orders; the third week they received 57 orders; the fourth week they received 92 orders. At this same rate, how many orders will they receive the sixth week?

NAME: _____ DATE: _____

THE BOWLING TOURNAMENT

In the intramural bowling tournament, there are 16 entries. The tournament is a single match elimination; that is, two bowlers compete at a time, and the loser is eliminated. How many games will be bowled to determine the champion?

NAME: _____ DATE: _____

SQUARES ON A CHECKERBOARD

How many squares are there on a standard 8 X 8 checkerboard?

NAME: _____   DATE: _____

CITY STREETS

Here is a map of the streets in a city. All of the streets are one way only as indicated by the arrows. How many different routes are there to go from City Hall (A) to the Municipal Ball Park (L)?

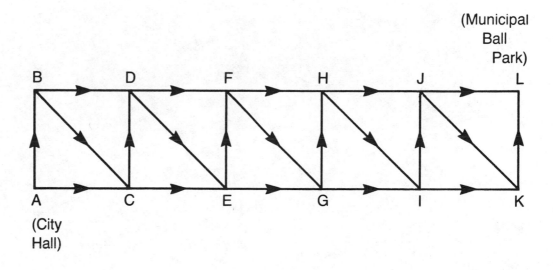

NAME: _____ DATE: _____

THE FERNANDO FAMILY VACATION TRIP

On a recent vacation trip, the Fernando family drove a total of 3,468 miles. Their car averaged 21.6 miles per gallon, and the average price of a gallon of gasoline was $1.37 9/10. How much did they spend for gasoline on the trip?

NAME: _____ DATE: _____

MOVING COINS

Place 20 pennies on the table in a row. Replace every fourth coin with a nickel. Now replace every third coin with a dime. Now replace every sixth coin with a quarter. What is the value of the 20 coins now on the table?

NAME: _____ DATE: _____

Place 20 pennies on the table in a row, with heads up. Now "flip" every coin to show tails. Now "flip" every other coin beginning with the second penny (2, 4, 6, . . .). Now flip every third coin, beginning with the third penny (3, 6, 9, . . .). Next flip every fourth penny, beginning with the fourth coin (4, 8, 12, . . .). Continue this procedure for 20 trials. Which pennies now have the heads up?

NAME: _____   DATE: _____

There are 20 students collecting golf balls that have fallen into the water trap, and selling them for practice balls. The first student brought in one golf ball. The second student then sold the ball. Student number three brought in three golf balls; student number four then sold one of them. Student number five brought in five golf balls; student number six sold one. Student number seven brought in seven golf balls; student number eight sold one. This continues—every odd-numbered student brings in the same number of golf balls as his or her number, while the even-numbered students sell one golf ball each. When all 20 students have done their thing, how many golf balls will be in the pile?

NAME: _____ DATE: _____

In a corner of the basement, Julie found an old rectangular fish tank frame; that is, the glass had been removed. An ant on one corner decides to crawl to the opposite corner. In how many different ways can the ant get to the opposite corner by walking along exactly three edges of the frame?

NAME: _____ DATE: _____

The new school has exactly 1,000 lockers and exactly 1,000 students. On the first day of school, the students meet outside the building and agree on the following plan: the first student will enter the school and open all of the lockers. The second student will then enter the school and close every locker with an even number (2, 4, 6, 8, . . .). The third student will then "reverse" every third locker (3, 6, 9, 12, . . .). That is, if the locker is closed, he will open it; if the locker is open, he will close it. The fourth student will then reverse every fourth locker, and so on until all 1,000 students in turn have entered the building and reversed the proper lockers. Which lockers will finally remain open?

NAME: _____ DATE: _____

GUESS TEST

Directions:

How good are you at guessing? Record your guesses for each of the following items.

1. How many times does your heart beat in one day?
2. What was the orbiting speed of the space shuttle Columbia?
3. How long does a light bulb burn?
4. How long is a new pencil?
5. What is the weight of a Datsun 210?
6. How many seats are there in the school auditorium?
7. What is the length of the longest beard every grown by a man?
8. How many words are there on a page in your dictionary?
9. What part of a typical 60 minute television show is devoted to commercials?
10. How many times does a wheel on a car revolve as it travels for one mile?
11. How far does the needle on a record player travel when a 12 inch LP record plays?

NAME: _____ DATE: _____

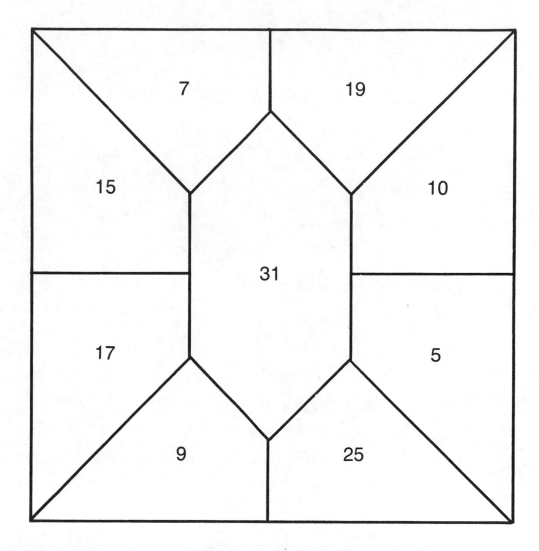

Mary hit the dartboard with four darts. Each dart hit a different number. Her total score was 60. How might she have scored 60?

NAME: _____ DATE: _____

Directions:

Fill in the empty circles on each side of the pentagon with the numbers from 1 to 10, so that the sum of the numbers on each side is 14.

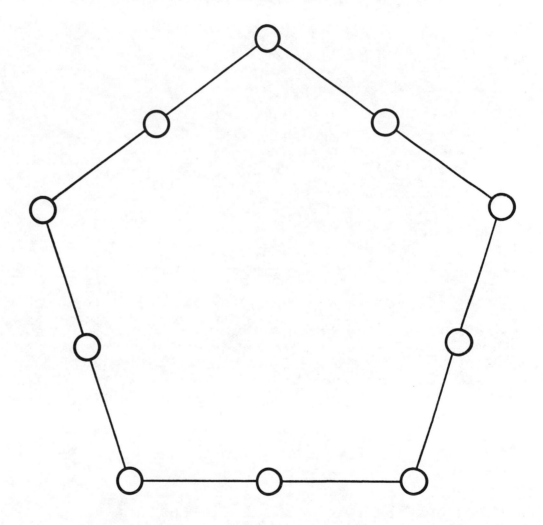

NAME: _____ DATE: _____

Leroy mailed some letters and postcards which cost him a total of $3.85 in postage. If each letter costs 20¢ and each postcard costs 13¢, how many of each did he mail?

NAME: _____ DATE: _____

Directions:

Replace each letter with a number from 0 through 9, so that the example is true. Each time a letter appears in the same problem, it must be replaced with the same number, and no two letters can have the same number replacement.

1. A D A M
    A N D
    E V E
      O N
        A
   —————
   R A F T

2.   S E N D
   + M O R E
  —————
   M O N E Y

3. $\dfrac{\text{T O P}}{\text{H A T}} = \text{H}$

4.   S U N
  + F U N
  —————
  S W I M

NAME: _____   DATE: _____

SYLLOGISMS

Directions:

For each pair of statements there is a conclusion drawn. Tell whether the conclusion is True, False, or Cannot be Determined.

1. Bob Jones owns a Chevrolet or a Ford.
   He does not own a Ford.
   Conclusion: Bob Jones owns a Chevrolet.   _____

2. Louise Ryan is in history class or biology class.
   She is not in biology.
   Conclusion: Louise Ryan is not in history class. _____

3. All canaries are yellow.
   Sal owns a canary.
   Conclusion: Sal's canary is blue.   _____

4. Some dogs are brown.
   Jeff owns a dog.
   Conclusion: Jeff's dog is white.   _____

5. All triangles have three sides.
   RST is a triangle.
   Conclusion: RST has three sides.   _____

6. All squares are rectangles.
   ABCD is a rectangle.
   Conclusion: ABCD is a square.   _____

7. Some styx live in Nyx.
   Pauline is a styx.
   Conclusion: Pauline lives in Nyx.   _____

8. All lupus are drus.
   John is a drus.
   Conclusion: John is a lupus.   _____

NAME: _____ DATE: _____

REASONING

Directions:

Below are two problems, each with four possible conclusions. Decide which of these are true, which of them are false, and which cannot be determined. Circle your choice for each.

1. All pro-basketball centers are over 6 foot 6 inches tall. Paul Rhodes is 6 foot 8 inches tall. Larry Werner is a pro-basketball center. So is Jerry Brown.

   (a) Larry Werner is over 6 foot 6 inches tall.   T   F   Unable to tell

   (b) Jerry Brown is 6 foot 3 inches tall.   T   F   Unable to tell

   (c) Paul Rhodes is a center.   T   F   Unable to tell

   (d) Paul and Larry are on the same basketball team.   T   F   Unable to tell

2. A gold record is a symbol of 1,000,000 copies sold. The Grasshoppers have seven gold records. The Bricks' latest record just went over the million mark in sales. The Canaries' most popular record sold 932,000 copies.

   (a) The Canaries have a gold record.   T   F   Unable to tell

   (b) The Bricks have a gold record.   T   F   Unable to tell

   (c) The three groups—the Grasshoppers, the Canaries and the Bricks—have a combined total of 15 gold records.   T   F   Unable to tell

   (d) The Grasshoppers record of the song "Nix" sold at least 1,000,000 copies.   T   F   Unable to tell

NAME: _____ DATE: _____

REASONING

Directions:

Below are two problems, each with four possible conclusions. Decide which of these are true, which of them are false, and which cannot be determined. Circle your choice for each.

1. A refreshment stand sells hot dogs for 75¢ each. Soft drinks are 50¢ each, while french fries cost 60¢ a portion.

   (a) John bought two hot dogs and received   T   F   Unable to
       change from a dollar bill.   tell

   (b) Matt received 30¢ change from a $5 bill.   T   F   Unable to
                                                               tell

   (c) Francine paid $1.25 for a hot dog and a soft   T   F   Unable to
       drink.   tell

   (d) At 4:00 p.m. the refreshment stand closed.   T   F   Unable to
                                                               tell

2. The Seminoles played the Navajos in high school basketball last night. The final score was Seminoles 58, Navajos 42.

   (a) The game went into overtime.   T   F   Unable to tell

   (b) The Seminoles won by 16 points.   T   F   Unable to tell

   (c) There were exactly 100 points scored in the game.   T   F   Unable to tell

   (d) The three top scorers on the Navajos each scored 17 points.   T   F   Unable to tell

NAME: _____ DATE: _____

DRAWING CONCLUSIONS

Four people—John, Mary, Roberta and Mike—own four cars: a Datsun, a Toyota, a Pontiac and a Ford.

1. John does not own a foreign-made car.
2. Mary went to the dance with the owner of the Toyota.
3. Mike owns the Ford.

1. What conclusion(s) can you draw from statement number 1?
    (a) John owns a Ford or a Pontiac.
    (b) John owns a Datsun or a Toyota.
    (c) John owns a Toyota.

2. What conclusion(s) can you draw from statements 1 and 2?
    (a) Mary owns the Pontiac.
    (b) Mary went to dinner with John.
    (c) Mary does not own a Toyota.

3. What conclusion(s) can you draw from statements 1 and 3?
    (a) Mary went to the dance with John.
    (b) John owns the Pontiac.
    (c) Roberta owns the Toyota.

4. What conclusion(s) can you draw from statements 1, 2, and 3?
    (a) Roberta owns the Toyota.
    (b) John owns the Pontiac.
    (c) Mary owns the Datsun.

NAME: _____ DATE: _____

DRAWING CONCLUSIONS

Susie, Nancy, Barbara and Claire each have a secret ambition. One of them wants to swim the English Channel, one wants to win the Indianapolis Stock Car Championship, one wants to run in the New York City Marathon, and one wants to win a gold medal for diving in the Olympics.

1. Claire can't drive.
2. Susie and Barbara won't go in the water.
3. Nancy is the swimmer.
4. Susie had dinner with the driver.

1. What conclusion(s) can you draw from statement number 1?
   (a) Barbara is the swimmer.
   (b) Claire can't win the Indianapolis Stock Car Championship.
   (c) Nancy is the diver.

2. What conclusion(s) can you draw from numbers 2 and 3?
   (a) Either Susie or Barbara is the runner.
   (b) Claire is the runner.
   (c) Nancy is the swimmer.

3. What conclusion(s) can you draw from numbers 1 and 3?
   (a) Claire is not the swimmer.
   (b) Nancy is the swimmer.
   (c) Barbara is the diver.

4. What conclusion(s) can you draw from numbers 1, 2, 3, and 4?
   (a) Barbara is the driver.
   (b) Claire is the diver.
   (c) Susie is the swimmer.

NAME: _____   DATE: _____

DETROIT DEMOLITION DERBY

Directions:

Read the given information and answer the question.

Three cars are left in the Detroit Demolition Derby: a 1976 Ford, a bright red Cadillac with a dented fender, and a blue Lincoln with a vinyl roof. The drivers are Bill, Charley, and Sue. Who is driving each car?

1. Sue drove into the Lincoln.
2. Sue said, "I'm going to get that Cadillac!"
3. Bill saw the Cadillac coming at him from the side
4. Charley saw the Ford hit the Lincoln.

Hint:

When information is presented in this manner, it is often helpful to organize the data in a chart, which is called a "matrix":

	Ford	Cadillac	Lincoln
Bill			
Sue			X
Charley			

As you read the problem and discover some facts, show them in the matrix. The first statement, "Sue drove into the Lincoln," tells us that Sue does not drive the Lincoln. Thus we have put an X to block out "Sue" and "Lincoln." The "X" shows that Sue cannot drive the Lincoln.

NAME: _____ DATE: _____

SWEET-TOOTH ICE CREAM PARLOR

Directions:

Read the given information and answer the question.

On the way home, George, Harry, Ina and Jan stopped at the Sweet-Tooth Ice Cream Parlor. They ordered the following items: a double-dip chocolate ice cream cone, a banana split, a strawberry milk shake, and a caramel sundae. Who had which one?

1. The boys are allergic to chocolate.
2. The caramel got stuck in George's braces.
3. Jan said, "I like bananas!"
4. Jan bought a chocolate ice cream cone and a strawberry milk shake for Ina and herself.
5. Ina shared some of what she had ordered with Harry.

NAME: _____ DATE: _____

MR. GEPETTO'S CLOCK SHOP

In Mr. Gepetto's Clock Shop, two cuckoo clocks were brought in for repairs. One clock has the cuckoo coming out every six minutes, while the other one has the cuckoo coming out every eight minutes. Both cuckoos come out at 12:00 noon. When will they both come out together again?

NAME: _____ DATE: _____

COWS AND DUCKS

A farmer has some ducks and cows in the field. He sends his two children, Nancy and Jeff, to count the number of animals. Jeff reports back that he counted 70 heads. Nancy counted 200 legs. How many of each kind were counted?

NAME: _____ DATE: _____

LISA'S GARDEN

Lisa bought 48 feet of fencing in order to make a rectangular garden. What dimensions should she use to obtain the largest area? (Consider only whole numbers of feet.)

NAME: _____ DATE: _____

SEEDING A LAWN

Mr. Chen wants to seed his front lawn. Grass seed is available in three pound boxes and five pound boxes. A three pound box costs $4.50, while a five pound box costs $6.58. Mr. Chen needs 17 pounds of seed. How many of each size box should he purchase to get the best buy?

NAME: _____   DATE: _____

JIMMY'S NUMBER TRICK

Jimmy was trying a number trick on Sandy. He told her to pick a number, add 5 to it, multiply the sum by 3, then subtract 10 and double the result. Sandy's final answer was 28. What number did she start with?

MARCY'S TAKE-HOME PAY

After receiving her weekly take-home pay, Marcy paid her roommate the $8 she owed for her share of the telephone bill. She then spent one-half of what was left on clothes, and then spent one-half of what was left on a concert ticket. She bought six stamps for 20¢ each, and had $12.10 left. What is her weekly take-home pay?

NAME: _____   DATE: _____

THE CARD GAME

Alice, Beth and Carol decide to play a game of cards. They agree on the following procedure: when a player loses a game, she will double the amount of money that each of the other players already has. First Alice loses a hand, and doubles the amount of money that Beth and Carol each have. Then Beth loses a hand and doubles the amount of money that Alice and Carol each have. Then Carol loses a hand and doubles the amount of money that Alice and Beth each have. They then decide to quit, and they find that each of them has exactly $8. How much did each of them start with?

NAME: _____   DATE: _____

WHAT'S MISSING?

Directions:

Sometimes a problem does not give you enough information. You must be able to tell what fact is missing. Read each of the following problems carefully. From the three statements given, select the one that is necessary to complete the solution.

1. Pete's Pet Palace is having a 25% sale on tropical fish. Janet buys guppies for her fishtank. How many can she buy for $2.85?

   What's Missing?

   _____ The number of guppies on sale
   _____ The amount of money Janet has to spend
   _____ The price of a guppy

2. Manuel bought dog food for his pet boxer, Bud. The dried dog food costs $8.95 for a twenty-five pound bag, while the moist dog food comes in 16-ounce cans. Manuel bought one twenty-five-pound bag and seven cans of the moist dog food. How much did he spend altogether?

   What's Missing?

   _____ The number of cans Manuel bought
   _____ The price he paid for the dried dog food
   _____ The price he paid for the cans of moist dog food

3. The most expensive coin ever sold at auction was sold for $272,000. The commission paid on the sale was $42,000. How much profit did the owner of the coin make on the sale?

   What's Missing?

   _____ The price the coin was sold for at the auction
   _____ The price the owner paid for the coin when he originally bought it
   _____ The amount of the commission

4. The Rams and the Cougars had a post-season tournament. The Rams established a new record by scoring 112 points. By how many points did they win?

What's Missing?

_____ How many points the Cougars scored
_____ How many points the Rams scored
_____ Where the game was played

5. The local donut shop is filling an order for the junior class prom, which will be held on Saturday evening. The donuts are packed 12 to a box. How many boxes are needed?

What's Missing?

_____ The price of each donut
_____ The weight of each donut
_____ The number of donuts ordered

6. The Pacific Record Club gives a new member five free records upon joining, provided they buy eight records during the first two years they are members. Each record costs $8.95. How many records did Dave receive in the two-year period?

What's Missing?

_____ How much each record costs
_____ How much Dave spent during the two years
_____ How many free records Dave received

7. The Barnes family took their vacation in the family camper. They traveled 1,250 miles. Mr. Barnes figures that he averaged eight miles to the gallon. How much did they spend for gas?

What's Missing?

_____ The number of gallons of gas they used
_____ The cost per gallon of gas
_____ The size of the camper

8. A plane leaves New York at 10:00 a.m. The flying time to its destination is four hours and twenty minutes. The plane travels at an average of 550 miles per hour ground speed. What is the local time when the plane lands?

What's Missing?

_____ The day of the flight
_____ Where the plane leaves from
_____ The time zone of the plane's destination

NAME: _____ DATE: _____

ROCK CONCERT ON METRON

Directions:

In each of the following problems, an additional fact is needed in order to complete the solution. Supply the missing fact.

1. On the planet Metron, the inhabitants have either two heads and three legs, or three heads and two legs. At a concert featuring the Metron Five Rock Group there were 5,000 available seats. The cost of each ticket is 250 Metron dollars. How much money was taken in at the concert?

   What's Missing? _____

2. The reporter for the local newspaper counted 13 heads in the President's box. How many Metronites were in the box?

   What's Missing? _____

3. The Metron Five played 22 numbers in the concert. The intermission lasted 1/2 hour. If the concert began at 8:00 local time, what time did it conclude?

   What's Missing? _____

4. It cost 8 Metron dollars to ride the monorail to the concert. Each monorail car holds 40 Metronites. Seven trains, each containing 14 cars, were used to transport some of the concert-goers. How much was collected on the monorail?

   What's Missing? _____

5. Evad bought the special souvenir program book. The book measures 8½ X 11 inches, and contains 30 photographs of the group. It also contains the autographs of each of the members of the group. Evad hopes to sell it for a profit of three Metron dollars. How much did he pay for the book?

   What's Missing? _____

6. At the refreshment stand, socats sell for 3½ Metron dollars, godtohs sell for four Metron dollars, and a drink of ados sells for two Metron dollars. If Evad bought some socats, some godtohs, and four ados, how much did he spend?

What's Missing? _____

NAME: _____ DATE: _____

HIDDEN QUESTIONS

Directions:

Sometimes there is a problem within a problem. That is, the problem contains a Hidden Question which must be answered in order to complete the solution. The problems below each contain a Hidden Question. State the Hidden Question, find its answer, and then complete the solution of the problem.

1. Luisa bought a hamburger for $1.65 and a soft drink for 69¢. How much change did she receive from a $5 bill?

   Hidden Question: _____

   Final Answer: _____

2. Jan bought five record albums at $6.95 each. She paid $1.15 in sales tax. How much did she spend altogether?

   Hidden Question: _____

   Final Answer: _____

3. Which is the better buy, a five-pound bag of potatoes for $1.59, or a 20-pound bag of potatoes for $6.00?

   Hidden Question: _____

   Final Answer: _____

4. Dr. L scored 22 points in last night's basketball game. He scored 13 field goals, and the rest in foul shots. How many foul shots did he make?

   Hidden Question: _____

   Final Answer: _____

5. Ramon has six fish tanks. Each tank requires five pounds of colored gravel. If the gravel costs 24¢ a pound, how much will Ramon spend on gravel?

Hidden Question: _____

Final Answer: _____

6. Admission to the Dog Show was $5 for adults and $3 for children. On Saturday, the show took in $6,000. If there were 900 adults present, how much was spent on children's tickets?

Hidden Questions: _____

Final Answer: _____

7. A four-woman relay team completed their race in 6 minutes and 58 seconds. The times for the first three runners were 1 minute 25 seconds, 1 minute 55 seconds and 2 minutes 15 seconds. What was the time for the final runner?

Hidden Question: _____

Final Answer: _____

8. Singin' Sam, the Record Man has 2½ hours of air time on his radio show. Commercials and chit-chat take up one hour of the time. If each record averages three minutes, how many records can he play?

Hidden Question: _____

Final Answer: _____

NAME: _____ DATE: _____

HIDDEN QUESTIONS

Directions:

Sometimes there is a problem within a problem. That is, the problem contains a Hidden Question which must be answered in order to complete the solution. The problems below each contain a Hidden Question. State the Hidden Question, find its answer, and then complete the solution of the problem.

1. Mr. Carter is paying off a $6,000 loan which he took out when he bought his new car. His monthly payments were set at $160. After he made 24 payments, he decided to pay-off the loan in full. How much did he still owe?

   Hidden Question: _____

   Final Answer: _____

2. The perimeter of a square is 80 centimeters. Find the area of the square.

   Hidden Question: _____

   Final Answer: _____

3. The gasoline tank on the Lawrence family's car contains 25 gallons of gasoline. On the highway, they average 22 miles per gallon. When they stopped for lunch, they had already travelled 350 miles. If the next gas station is 180 miles away, can they make it without running out of gas?

   Hidden Question: _____

   Final Answer: _____

4. A 12-ounce can of orange juice concentrate is used together with three cans of water to make orange juice. Is a 42-ounce container large enough to hold the mixture?

   Hidden Question: _____

   Final Answer: _____

5. The Noise rock group recorded 15 songs last year. Of these, 20% became million sellers. How many records that they recorded last year did not become million sellers?

   Hidden Question: _____

   Final Answer: _____

6. A leaky faucet drips one drop of water every second. If it takes ten drops of water to make a milliliter, how much water is lost in a 24-hour period of time?

   Hidden Question: _____

   Final Answer: _____

7. An airplane takes off from Philadelphia Airport for Los Angeles at 9:00 a.m. and travels at a ground speed of 550 miles per hour. At the same time, another plane takes off from New York and flies to Las Vegas, at 525 miles per hour. The distance from Philadelphia to Los Angeles is 2560 miles, while the distance from New York to Las Vegas is 2150 miles. Which plane lands first?

   Hidden Question: _____

   Final Answer: _____

8. Sherm is filling an order for 1,000 cupcakes. Each box contains 12 cupcakes. Before he breaks for lunch, he filled 40 boxes. How many cupcakes must he box after his lunch to complete the order?

   Hidden Question: _____

   Final Answer: _____

NAME: _____   DATE: _____

MULTI-STAGE PROBLEMS

Directions:

The problems that follow contain more than one step. Look for the Hidden Questions. It is necessary to answer these before you can complete the solution.

1. The length of a rectangle is 12 centimeters, and its perimeter is 34 centimeters. What is the area of the rectangle?

2. Ronald bought seven rolls of film at the local camera shop. What is the least amount he could have spent on the film?

FILM SALE	
Each Roll	$ 3.20
Five Rolls	$15.00

3. Mike has two pieces of wire fencing, each 5½ meters long. He also has three pieces of wooden fencing, each 2½ meters long. How much longer is the wire fencing than the wooden fencing?

4. Last weekend, the stamp show took in $12,000 in admissions. Tickets costs $5 for adults and $3 for children. There were 1800 adult tickets sold. Were there 900 children in attendance?

5. Amy had 12 postcards and 14 first-class letters to mail. It costs 20¢ to mail each letter and 13¢ to mail each postcard. She had $4 with her. Did she have enough money to mail the postcards and the letters?

6. A balloon is floating at 2,000 feet. At what time should they start their descent if they want to land at 1:15 p.m., and the rate of descent is 100 feet per minute?

NAME: _____ DATE: _____

MULTI-STAGE PROBLEMS

Directions:

The problems that follow contain more than one step. Look for the Hidden Questions. It is necessary to answer these before you can complete the solution.

1. Barbara and Arlene were planning a sweet sixteen party for their cousin, Jan. At the delicatessen counter they bought 2½ pounds of potato salad at 69¢ a pound, 1½ pounds of salami at $2.49 a pound, and 1½ pounds of roast beef at $3.50 a pound. How much did they spend for these items?

2. A long distance telephone call from Atlanta to Sante Fe costs $1.05 for the first three minutes and 23¢ for each additional minute. When the phone bill came, the charge for the call that Jane made to her friend Allison was $4.27. For how long did they talk?

3. The eighth grade class at Ferriss Junior High School is taking a class trip to the local planetarium. They expect to use school buses and parent-driven automobiles for transportation. Each bus seats 27 people including the driver and each car carries four people plus the driver. They used five cars and four buses. All the seats were filled except for seven in the last bus. How many people went on the trip to the planetarium?

4. Stan is building a wall of cinder blocks that will measure 8 feet high and 100 feet long. The mortar used to hold the cinder blocks in place occupies 5% of the total area. If the face area of each cinder block is 120 square inches, how many cinder blocks are needed for the wall?

5. Rori is building a totem pole that will stand at the entrance to Camp Shining Lake. The totem pole consists of six heads of animals, each

half the size of the one below it. If the bottom head is four feet high, how high will the entire totem pole be when Rori finishes it?

6. A swimming pool with a level bottom is in the form of a rectangle that is 60 feet long and 20 feet wide. Jeremy decided to raise the water level in the pool one foot. If there are 7.5 gallons of water per cubic foot, how many gallons did he add?

NAME: _____ DATE: _____

NUMBER REPLACEMENTS

Directions:

Write the number that you would use to replace each of the following numbers in estimating the results of a computation. The first four have been done for you.

	Number	*Replacement*
1.	.87	<u>1</u>
2	37	<u>4</u>0
3.	234	<u>2</u>00
4.	1,110	<u>1</u>,000
5.	3.2	_.0
6.	65	_0
7.	127	_00
8.	7	_0
9.	1,235	_,000
10.	25,642	_0,000
11.	978	_,000
12.	837	_00
13.	3,654	_,000
14.	42	_0

NAME: _____ DATE: _____

APPROXIMATE ANSWERS

Directions:

Find the approximate answer to the following problems. Use a calculator to check your estimate.

1. $68 \times 82 =$

   $68 \rightarrow 70$
   $82 \rightarrow 80$
   $\overline{5600}$

   $$
   \begin{array}{r}
   82 \\
   \times\ \ 68 \\
   \hline
   656 \\
   492\ \ \\
   \hline
   5576
   \end{array}
   $$

2. $3876 + 5121 =$

   $3876 \rightarrow \underline{\ }000$
   $+ 5121 \rightarrow \underline{\ 000}$

3. $286 - 43 =$

   $286 \rightarrow \underline{\ }00$
   $- 43 \rightarrow \underline{\ \ 0}$

4. $537 \div 48 =$

   $537 \rightarrow \underline{\ }00$
   $48 \rightarrow \underline{\ \ 0}$

5. $36.5 \times 87.7 =$

   $36.5 \rightarrow \underline{\ }0.0$
   $\times 87.7 \rightarrow \underline{\ 0.0}$

6. $732 + 87 + 256 =$

   $732 \rightarrow \underline{\ }00$
   $87 \rightarrow \underline{\ \ 0}$
   $256 \rightarrow \underline{\ }00$

NAME: _____ DATE: _____

APPROXIMATE ANSWERS

Directions:

Find the approximate answer to each of the following problems. Then use a calculator to check your estimate.

1. 320
   713
   <u>878</u>

2. 89.3
   37.9
   <u>54.8</u>

3.   3,281
   −   756

4.   87,562
   − 21,818

5. 86.3 × 125.4

6. 4,325 × 3,812

7. 57.8 ÷ 6.2 =

8. 87.4 ÷ 28.3 =

NAME: _____   DATE: _____

SUPERMARKET SHOPPING

Directions:

Estimate how much each of the following shopping lists would cost on a trip to the local supermarket. Then compute the actual costs and compare.

	Your estimate	*Actual cost*
I.		
2 jars of peanut butter at 97¢ each	_____	_____
3 cans of string beans at 37¢ each	_____	_____
2 bottles of soda at two for 49¢	_____	_____
Total:	_____	_____
II.		
2 packages of jello at 21¢ each	_____	_____
2 cans of fruit cocktail at 43¢ each	_____	_____
1 can of spaghetti sauce at $1.12	_____	_____
2 boxes of spaghetti at 63¢ each	_____	_____
1 package of ground cheese at 73¢	_____	_____
Total:	_____	_____
III.		
1 box of dishwashing detergent at $1.49	_____	_____
3 cakes of soap at 57¢ each	_____	_____
2 cans of tuna fish at 92¢ each	_____	_____
4 cans of soda at two for 49¢	_____	_____
3 gallons of ice cream at $1.89 each	_____	_____
Total:	_____	_____

IV.

7 grapefruits at 19¢ each   _____   _____

3 pounds of apples at 27¢ a pound   _____   _____

3 cans of sardines at 43¢ each   _____   _____

2 packages of pretzels at 52¢ each   _____   _____

5 pounds of sugar at 43¢ a pound   _____   _____

2 bags of potato chips at 39¢ each   _____   _____

Total: _____   _____

V.

2 quarts of milk at 59¢ each   _____   _____

1 pint of sour cream at 32¢   _____   _____

2 packages of cream cheese at 39¢ each   _____   _____

1 loaf of bread at 72¢   _____   _____

2 cans of shaving cream at $1.29 each   _____   _____

2 packs of razor blades at $1.95 each   _____   _____

Total: _____   _____

VI.

3 pounds of salami at $1.49 a pound   _____   _____

2 pounds of roast turkey at $1.95 a pound   _____   _____

2 pounds of potato salad at 72¢ a pound   _____   _____

2 pounds of tomatoes at 39¢ a pound   _____   _____

2 heads of lettuce at 74¢ a head   _____   _____

1 bag of potato chips at 59¢   _____   _____

Total: _____   _____

NAME: _____ DATE: _____

ESTIMATING ANSWERS

Directions:

Read each of the following problems and estimate the answer. Three estimates are given for each problem. Choose the one that you think is closest to the actual answer.

1. From Philadelphia to Atlantic City is a distance of 58 miles. Eileen and her family left Philadelphia at 8:15 a.m. and arrived in Atlantic City at 10:15 a.m. About how fast did they travel?

   (a) 20 miles per hour   (b) 30 miles per hour   (c) 40 miles per hour

2. A builder uses 585 bricks to build a foundation for a garage. How many bricks will he need in order to build 11 garages?

   (a) 6,000   (b) 8,000   (c) 10,000

3. Coffee beans are packed in sacks that hold approximately 95 pounds. Juanita is shipping 1,825 sacks of coffee beans. How many pounds are in the shipment?

   (a) 120,000   (b) 150,000   (c) 180,000

4. A spring releases 28 gallons of sparkling water per minute into the lake. How many gallons of water would be deposited in the lake in 8 hours?

   (a) 2,000   (b) 18,000   (c) 50,000

5. The Millers went to a local restaurant for dinner last night. Three people ordered lasagna at $5.95 each, two people ordered scallopini at $8.95 each, two ordered shrimp scampi at $9.25, and one ordered a pizza for $4.25. Approximately how much was the total bill?

   (a) $50   (b) $60   (c) $70

NAME: _____ DATE: _____

ESTIMATING ANSWERS

Directions:

Read each of the problems on the sheet. First estimate the answer. Then solve the problem and compare the actual answer with your original estimate.

1. A taxi ride from Janet's house to the Senior Prom costs $7.75, and she gives the driver a $1 tip. How much change should she receive from a $20 bill?

2. We are going to take the entire high school band to a football game next week. The band has 270 members and each bus holds 37 people. How many buses do we need to transport the band?

3. Jeff bought two records that cost $7.95 each and three notebooks that cost 95¢ each. He has a $20 bill in his pocket. How much will Jeff spend?

4. The junior high school is preparing to give the standardized tests in a few weeks, and they want to order pencils. They need 29 pencils for each class, and there are 28 classes in the school. How many boxes of pencils should they order if pencils come a dozen in a box?

5. The distance that the Canadian goose flies from Canada to its winter retreat in Texas is about 2,870 miles. If the Canadian goose can cover about 190 miles a day, how many days will it take to reach Texas from Canada?

6. The local movie theater charges $1.95 for children and $3.95 for adults. Last night there were 48 children and 17 adults at the show. How much money was collected?

7. Before leaving on a camping trip, the Jonas family wishes to buy some new camping supplies. They need two sleeping bags that sell for $24.98 each, two cooking kits that sell for $19.98 each, and a pup tent that sells for $17.75. How much money will the supplies cost?

8. A computer prorammer usually earns $11.95 an hour, and loses approximately 1/3 in deductions. If Annie works a 39-hour week, how much money will she take home?

9. John wants to tile the floor in his recreation room. He will use tiles that are 1 foot by 1 foot square, and come 48 in a box. If his recreation room is 27 feet by 12 feet, how many boxes of tiles will John order to do the job?

NAME: _____ DATE: _____

WHICH MAKES THE MOST SENSE?

Directions:

Each of the questions below is followed by several choices. Circle the choice which makes the most sense.

1. Bonnie and Clyde had lunch together in the school cafeteria, last Tuesday. How much did each one spend?

   (a) $1.85   (b) $5.75   (c) $20.00

2. Stan is in the eighth grade. How old is he?

   (a) 5 years old   (b) 9 years old   (c) 13 years old

3. The Johnson family consists of the two parents, three children, a dog and a cat. How many cars do the Johnsons own?

   (a) 2   (b) 20   (c) 200

4. Janet walks to school every morning from her house. How long does it take her?

   (a) 2 minutes   (b) 20 minutes   (c) 2 hours

5. Juanita loves music, so for her birthday her parents bought her a new record player. How much did they spend?

   (a) $250   (b) $2.50   (c) $2500

6. Ken is a movie buff. He loves the movies. How many movies did he see last Thursday?

   (a) 2   (b) 22   (c) 222

7. Jaimie came to school to take her standardized tests last Friday. How many pencils did she bring with her?

   (a) 30   (b) 13   (c) 3

8. Jerry had to know how much his full grown St. Bernard dog weighs in order to buy a license. How much did the dog weigh?

   (a) 125 pounds   (b) 300 pounds   (c) 400 pounds

NAME: _____ DATE: _____

DOES THE ANSWER MAKE SENSE?

Directions:

Below are nine problems that appeared on an 8th grade math test. Each one is followed by an answer that was given by one of the students. Tell whether the answer makes sense. Then solve the problem and see if you were right.

1. Sales tax in Pennsylvania is 6%. Jeff bought a new car for $8,200. How much was the sales tax?

   Student's Answer: ____$492____ *Does It Make Sense?* _____

2. Jaimie scored 75, 80, and 85 on her three math tests this marking period. What was her average?

   Student's Answer: ____40____ *Does It Make Sense?* _____

3. We can put 25 students on a school bus. How many busses do we need to take all 575 students on a field trip to the museum?

   Student's Answer: __157 busses__ *Does It Make Sense?* _____

4. A 20 foot length of rope costs $20. At the same rate, how much does an 80 foot length of the same rope cost?

   Student's Answer: ____$50____ *Does It Make Sense?* _____

5. Mrs. Jackson jogs 2½ miles each day. How much does she jog in a week?

   Student's Answer: __21 miles__ *Does It Make Sense?* _____

6. On a shelf in the local ice cream store there are 9 boxes of ice cream cones. Each box contains 12 cones. There are 5 more cones on the counter. How many cones are there altogether?

   Student's Answer: __213 cones__ *Does It Make Sense?* _____

7. Mike bought a new Rolling Stones record album for $7.65. He gave the clerk a ten dollar bill and 65¢ in coins. How much change did Mike receive?

   Student's Answer: ____$3.00____ *Does It Make Sense?* _____

8. Roberta just bought several stereo components. She bought two speakers at $175 each, a turntable for $225, and an amplifier for $325. How much did she spend for the equipment?

Student's Answer: ____$725____ *Does It Make Sense?* _____

9. The school drama club put on a production of *My Fair Lady*. It ran for 2 nights and was a sell-out both nights. The first night the audience consisted of 650 adults and 350 children. On the second night there were 700 adults and 300 children. Tickets for adults were $4, and tickets for children were $2. How much did the school receive for admissions on the two nights?

Student's Answer· ____$5,350____ *Does It Make Sense?* _____ __

NAME: _____ DATE: _____

FIND THE ERROR

Directions:

Below are 8 problems that appeared on a math test. Each is followed by an answer that was given by a student. The answer is wrong! See if you can tell where the student made the error.

1. The grades for Lucy's math tests were 75, 65 82 and 74. What was Lucy's average for the four tests?

   Student's Answer: _____69_____   *Error:* Lucy added incorrectly. She got 276 as her sum instead of 296.
   $276 \div 4 = 69$
   $296 \div 4 = 74$, the correct answer.

2. Jeremy is a salesman for a furniture company. He receives a commission of 5% of his sales. Last month his total sales amounted to $40,000. What was his commission?

   Student's Answer: _____$20,000_____   *Error:* _____

3. Andy bought 3/4 of a pound of cashew nuts and 3/4 of a pound of salted peanuts to make a nut mix. He added 1/2 of a pound of raisins. What was the total weight of the mixture?

   Student's Answer: _____7/10 pound_____   *Error:* _____

4. Sally spent $3.78 on canned orange juice which costs 42¢ a can. How many cans did she buy?

   Student's Answer: _____90 cans_____   *Error:* _____

5. Yesterday, the Donut Heaven Donut Shop produced 5,280 donuts. They packed their donuts in boxes of twelve. How many boxes did they use yesterday?

   Student's Answer: _____44_____   *Error:* _____

6. During the past season, the Baltimore Blue Hens semi-pro football team scored 18 touchdowns (6 points each), 13 points-after-touchdown (1 point each), 11 field goals (3 points each) and two safeties (2 points each). How many points did they score altogether?

   Student's Answer: _____118_____ *Error:* _____

7. On an inter-galactic space mission, the space ship Vulcan traveled 832,471 miles the first week, 268,947 miles the second week, and 1,756,088 miles the third week. How far did it travel during the three weeks?

   Student's Answer: ___12,770,268___ *Error:* _____

8. Gasoline costs $1.24^{9/10} a gallon. On a recent trip the Chen family used 87 gallons of gas. How much did they spend on gas for the trip?

   Student's Answer: ____10.87____ *Error:* _____

NAME: _____ DATE: _____

VARIETY TIC-TAC-TOE GAME BOARDS

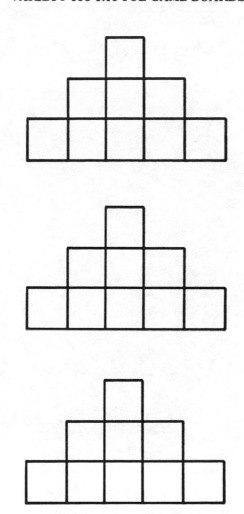

NAME: _____ DATE: _____

VARIETY TIC-TAC-TOE GAME BOARDS

VARIETY TIC-TAC-TOE GAME BOARDS

NAME: _____ DATE: _____

9-CELL TIC-TAC-TOE GAME BOARD

NAME: _____ DATE: _____

LINE TIC-TAC-TOE GAME BOARD

•
•
•
•
•
•
•
•
•
•
•
•
•
•

NAME: _____ DATE: _____

5 × 5 TIC-TAC-TOE GAME BOARD

NAME: _____ DATE: _____

CROSS-'EM-OUT TIC-TAC-TOE GAME BOARD

NAME: _____   DATE: _____

13-CELL TIC-TAC-TOE GAME BOARD

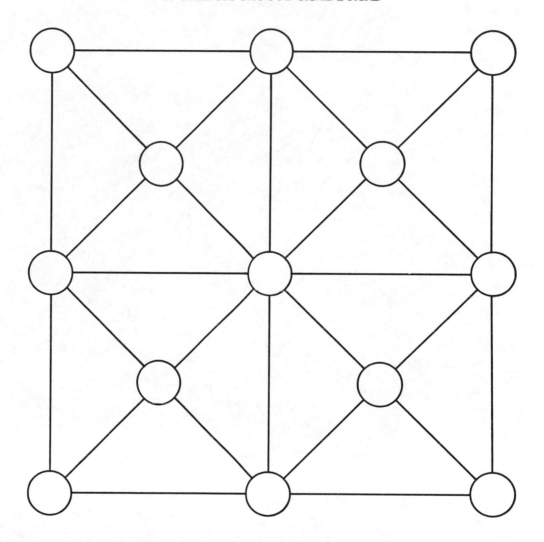

NAME: _____ DATE: _____

TRIANGULAR TIC-TAC-TOE GAME BOARD

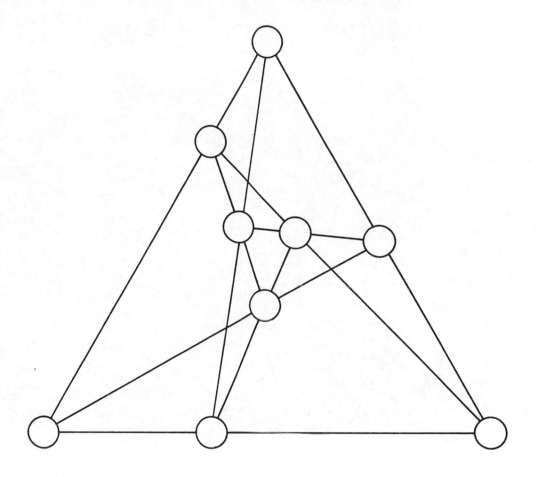

NAME: _____ DATE: _____

SPIRAL TIC-TAC-TOE GAME BOARD

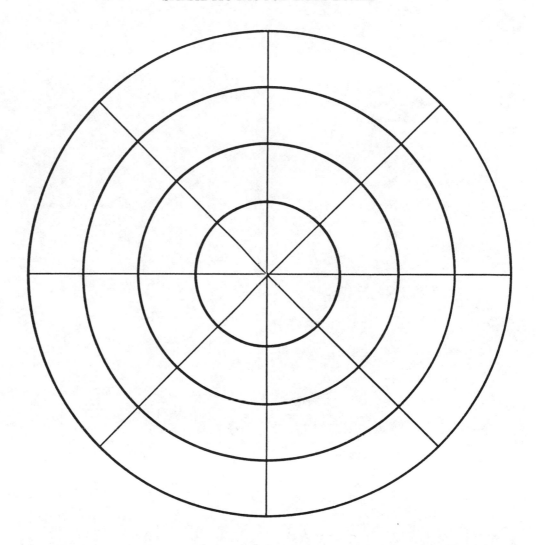

NAME: _____ DATE: _____

STANDARD 8 × 8 CHECKERBOARD

TRIANGULAR CHECKERS GAME BOARD

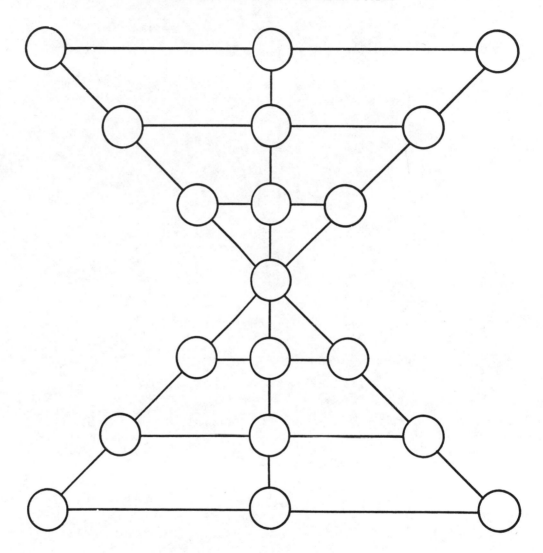

NAME: _____ DATE: _____

CIRCULAR CHECKERS GAME BOARD

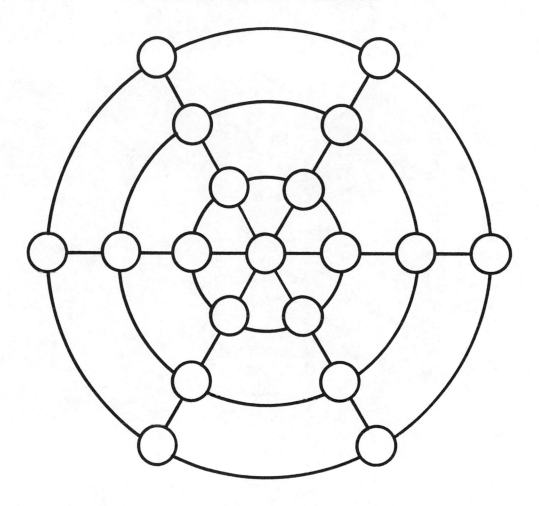

NAME: _____ DATE: _____

5 × 5 CHECKERS GAME BOARD

NAME: _____ **DATE:** _____

MAKING BRIDGES GAME BOARD

```
                              ( O's )

         o         o         o         o         o
    x         x         x         x         x         x
         o         o         o         o         o
    x         x         x         x         x         x
         o         o         o         o         o
( X's )  x    x    x    x    x    x   ( X's )
         o         o         o         o         o
    x         x         x         x         x         x
         o         o         o         o         o
    x         x         x         x         x         x
         o         o         o         o         o

                              ( O's )
```

NAME: _____ DATE: _____

TWO-WAY TRAFFIC GAME BOARD

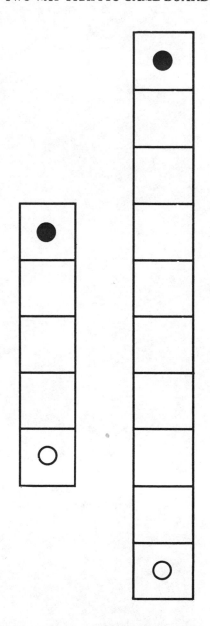

WANDERING ROOKS GAME BOARD

NAME: _____ DATE: _____

FOUR-COLOR GAME BOARD

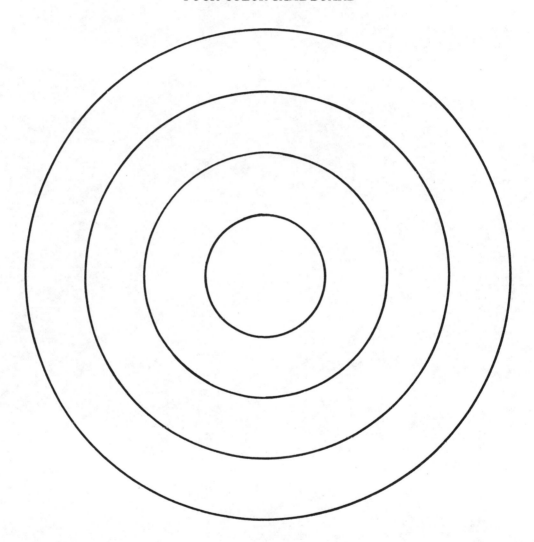

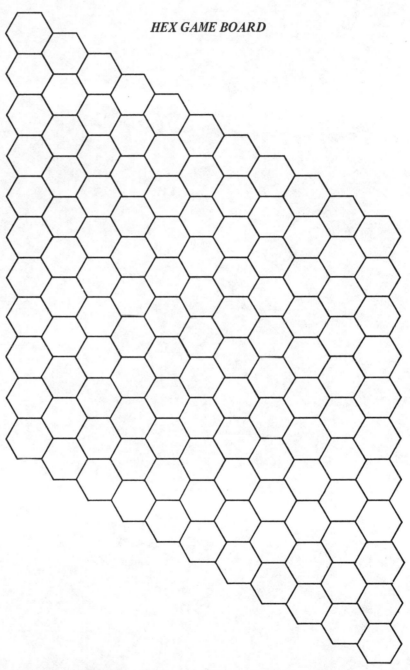

HEX GAME BOARD

NAME: _____   DATE: _____

Problem:

Circle two numbers whose quotient is 8.

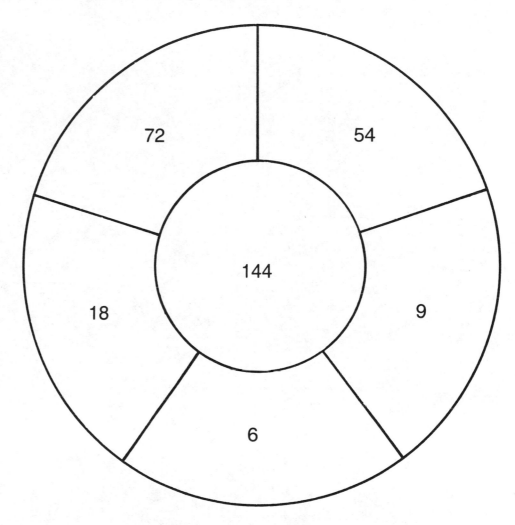

NAME: _____ DATE: _____

Problem:

Find all of the two digit numbers for which the sum of the two digits is 10.

NAME: _____ DATE: _____

Problem:

A spider wishes to crawl from point H to point B. How many different "trips" can he crawl, if each trip is exactly three edges long?

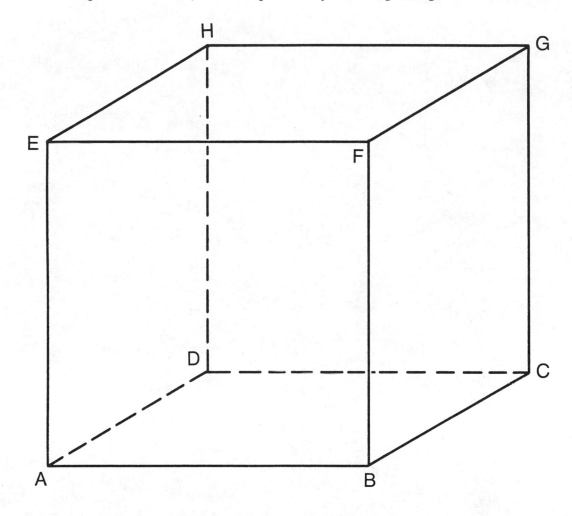

NAME: _____   DATE: _____

Problem:

I have five coins: quarters, nickels and dimes. The total value of the coins is 50¢. How many of each do I have?

Problem:

The six students in Mr. Charne's biology class were arranged numerically around a hexagonal table. What number student was opposite student number 4?

NAME: _____ DATE: _____

Problem:

Jim is in line at the bridge waiting to pay his toll. He counts four cars in front of him and six cars behind him. How many cars are there in line at the bridge?

Problem:

The listed price of *Sports Magazine* is $1.25 a copy. You pay $16.56 for a 24-issue subscription. How much do you save by buying the subscription?

NAME: _____ **DATE:** _____

Problem:

Last Saturday, George and his friend Mike went to a big-league baseball game. After the game, they went to the locker room to collect autographs of their favorite players. Together they collected eighteen autographs, but Mike collected four more than George. How many did George collect?

Problem:

Norene had set her wristwatch when she left for school at exactly 7:30 a.m. on Monday. At 1:30 p.m. on Monday, she noticed that her watch had lost 4 minutes. At this same rate, how many minutes will the watch lose by the time Norene resets it when she leaves for school at 7:30 a.m. on Tuesday?

NAME: _____ DATE: _____

Problem:

The faces of a cube are numbered with consecutive numbers. Three of the numbers are shown. What is the sum of the numbers on all the faces of the cube?

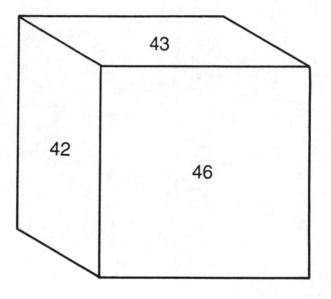

Problem:

Laura jogs seven blocks the first day of her training program. She increases her distance by two blocks each day. On the last day, she jogs 25 blocks. How many days was she in training?

Problem:

The town of Graphville has intersections formed by 27 avenues that run north-south, and 31 streets that run east-west. If we plan one traffic light at each intersection, how many traffic lights do we need?

NAME: _____   DATE: _____

Problem:

How much will it cost to cut a log into eight pieces if cutting it into four equal pieces costs 60¢? (There is no stacking of the pieces.)

Problem:

My license tag is a three-digit number. The product of the digits is 216, their sum is 19, and the numbers appear in ascending order. Find my license plate number.

NAME: _____ DATE: _____

Problem:

Mr. Lopez' class collected $5.29 for a class gift. Each student contributed the same amount, and each paid with the same five coins. How many dimes were collected?

Problem:

A fancy bottle of perfume costs $25. The bottle can be purchased by collectors without the perfume. When purchased this way, the bottle costs $15 less than the perfume. How much does the bottle cost alone?

Problem:

In a recent sale at the local stationery store, the following sign appeared:

```
ERASERS  5¢
PENCILS  7¢
LIMIT:  3  OF  EACH  TO  A
CUSTOMER
```

If you had 20¢ to spend, what different combinations of pencils and erasers could you buy?

NAME: _____ DATE: _____

Problem:

The Kudin family is putting a fence around their garden which is in the shape of a square. If there will be seven fence posts on each side of the square, how many posts are there altogether?

Problem:

Replace each of the question marks with the same number so that the fractions will be equivalent. What is the number?

$$\frac{2}{?} = \frac{?}{32}$$

NAME: _____   DATE: _____

Problem:

The Iowa Falcons and the Indiana Bombers set a new semi-pro league record last week when they scored 362 points between them in one game. If the Falcons lost by 14 points, how many points did the Bombers score?

Problem:

To help earn some spending money in school, Ruth bought some Indian Head pennies at 6 for $10, and then sold them at 4 for $10. She made a total of $50 profit. How many pennies did she buy and sell?

NAME: _____ **DATE:** _____

Problem:

Fill in the following figure with the digits from 1 through 8 so that no consecutive numbers have a point or a side in common.

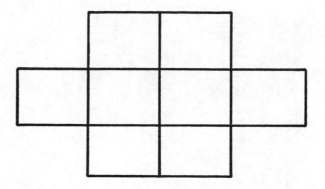

Problem:

Jason computed his average for five tests in his math class, and found that he had a 76. What must he score on the final two tests in order to raise his average to 80?

NAME: _____ DATE: _____

Problem:

A man takes a 5,000 mile trip in his car. He rotates his tires (4 on the car and 1 spare) so that at the end of the trip each tire had been used for the same number of miles. How many miles were driven on each tire?

Problem:

A 42 ounce can of Fruity Drink contains 7 ounces of pure fruit juice, and the remainder is water and additives. If Georgette drinks 6 ounces of the fruit drink, how much pure fruit juice does she consume?

NAME: _____ DATE: _____

Problem:

There are four numbers less than 1,000 that are both perfect squares and also perfect cubes. Find them.

Problem:

Linda is playing "Guess My Number" with her classmates. See if you can find her number from the following clues:

1. her number is a multiple of 5;
2. it is less than 200;
3. it is divisible by 3;
4. its ten's digit equals the sum of its other two digits.

NAME: _____ DATE: _____

Problem:

A stadium holds 100,000 people. Ushers estimated that 3 males came in for every 2 females. How many males and how many females were in the stadium?

Problem:

When Sue puts marbles in boxes by 2s, she has one left over. If she puts them in the boxes by 3s, she has one left over. And, if she puts them in by 5s, she still has one left over. What is the smallest number of marbles she can use to do this?

NAME: _____ DATE: _____

Problem:

Find a number that when multiplied by 81 or divided into 6,561 gives the same answer.

Problem:

A neighborhood pet shop sells only dogs and birds. One morning they count a total of 10 heads and 34 legs. How many dogs and how many birds do they have?

NAME: _____ DATE: _____

Problem:

It costs a dime to cut and weld a chain-link. What is the minimum number of cuts needed to make a single chain from seven individual links?

Problem:

Jeff has a record collection. If he stacks them in piles of seven, he has no records left over. But, when he puts them into piles of 2, 3, or 4, he always has one record left over. What is the minimum number of records Jeff has in his collection?

NAME: _____ DATE: _____

Problem:

In the outer reaches of space, there are eleven relay stations for the Inter-galactic Space Ship Line. There are space ship routes between the relay stations as shown on the map.

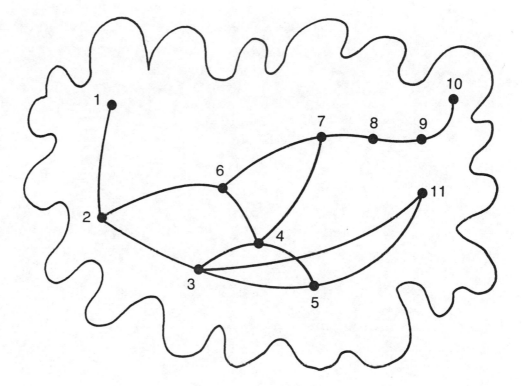

Eleven people have been engaged as communications operators, one for each station. The people are Alex, Barbara, Cindy, Donna, Elvis, Frances, Gloria, Hal, Irene, Johnny and Karl. The two people in the stations with connecting routes will be talking to each other a great deal, to discuss the space ships that fly from station to station. It would be helpful if these people were friendly to each other. Here are the pairs of people who are friends:

Alex–Barbara	Hal–Frances	Irene–Karl
Gloria–Johnny	Gloria–Irene	Donna–Elvis
Donna–Irene	Alex–Gloria	Karl–Elvis
Cindy–Hal	Alex–Donna	Johnny–Irene
Johnny–Cindy	Donna–Karl	

Place the eleven people in the eleven stations so that the people in connecting stations are friends.

NAME: _____ DATE: _____

Problem:

Stan, Stu, Sam, Shirley and Selma were the first five finishers of the seventeen-mile road race. From the given clues, give the order in which they finished.

1. Stan passed Stu just before the finish line.
2. Selma finished 10 seconds ahead of Stan.
3. Shirley crossed the finish line in a dead heat with Stu.
4. Sam was fifth at the finish.

NAME: _____ **DATE:** _____

Problem:

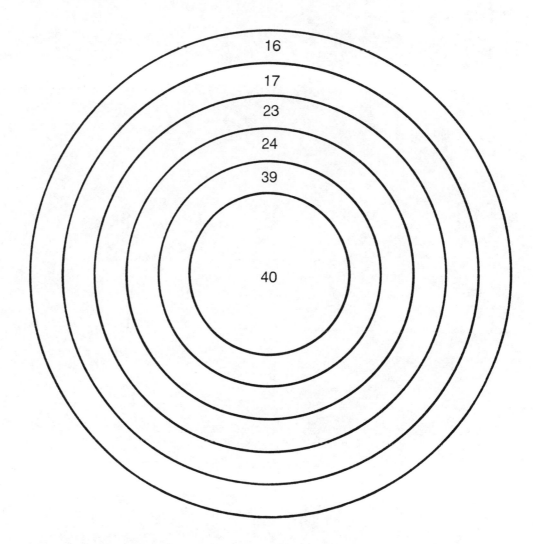

How many arrows will it take to hit the target and score exactly 100?

NAME: _____ DATE: _____

Problem:

Current postal rates for a first class letter are 20¢ for the first ounce or fraction thereof, and 17¢ for each additional ounce or fraction.

1. How much would it cost to mail a first class letter that weighs 3½ ounces?

2. A first class letter was mailed and cost $1.05 in postage. What did it weigh?

NAME: _____   DATE: _____

Problem:

I just came back from four marble games. I have only 21 marbles left. In the first game, I lost one-half of my marbles. In the second game I won 12 times what I had. I won 9 more marbles in the third game. But in the fourth game, the game was a draw and no marbles were exchanged. I forgot how many marbles I began with. Can you tell me how many I had when I started?

NAME: _____ DATE: _____

Problem:

Steve is responsible for keeping the fish tanks in the Seaside Aquarium Shop filled with water. One of their 50-gallon tanks has a small leak and, along with evaporation, loses 2 gallons of water each day. Every three days, Steve adds 5 gallons of water to the tank, and on the 30th day he fills it. How much water will he have to add on the 30th day to fill the tank?

NAME: _____ DATE: _____

Problem:

The numbers on the uniforms of the Granville Baseball Team all consist of two digits. Two friends on the team are also amateur mathematicians. They select their numbers so the square of the sum of their numbers is the same as the four-digit number formed by their uniforms when they stand side by side. What are the numbers on their uniforms?

NAME: _____ DATE: _____

Problem:

The license plate on my car contains five different digits. My son installed it upside down, yet it still shows a five-digit number. The only thing is, the new number exceeds the original number by 63,783. What was the original number on the license plate?

NAME: _____   **DATE:** _____

Problem:

Four couples play bridge every month. The wives' names are Gladys, Hariett, Susan and Bonnie. The husband's names are Marv, Allan, Steve and Herb (but not in that order). Who is married to whom?

1. Marv is Susan's brother.
2. Susan and Herb were engaged, but broke up when Herb met his present wife.
3. Bonnie has two brothers, but her husband is an only child.
4. Gladys is married to Steve.

NAME: _____   DATE: _____

Problem:

How many solutions can you find for R and S that satisfy the equation?

$$\frac{R}{S} + \frac{S}{R} = 2$$

Problem:

Find the smallest perfect square of three digits such that the sum of these digits is not a perfect square.

NAME: _____   DATE: _____

Problem:

How many triangles are there in this figure?

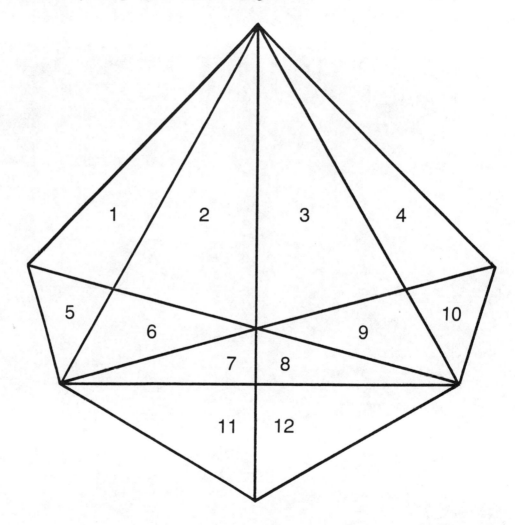